Jewish History in the Bible Portrayed in Coins

Dr. John G. Leslie

Jewish History in the Bible Portrayed in Coins

Copyright © 2016, 2004   John G. Leslie

Most photographs are taken by John G. Leslie; photos taken by others are indicated either in footnotes, captions, or acknowledgements, along with permission to use them.

Scripture quotations taken from the New American Standard Bible® (NASB),
Copyright © 1960, 1962, 1963, 1968, 1971, 1972, 1973,
1975, 1977, 1995 by The Lockman Foundation
Used by permission. www.Lockman.org

All rights reserved.

ISBN-10: 0692706305
ISBN-13: 978-0692706305 (Deluge Press)

Cover photograph by John G. Leslie

DELUGE PRESS
Gallup, New Mexico

CONTENTS

	Acknowledgments	v
1	Introduction	1
2	History of Barter before Coins in the Middle East: Use of Emblems; Jewish Pre-Coinage	2
3	Development of Coin Stamping in the Middle East: Review of History of the Region	6
4	Daniel's Dream: Division of Mankind in Relationship to the Jewish People and the Merneptah Stele	10
5	Times of the Jews upon Return from Babylon During the Persian Period and Transition to the Greek Period	18
6	History of the Hasmonean Rise to Power in Judea	22
7	The Roman Period in Judea and Surrounding Area: The Herods with Antipater (and the Idumaeans) Roman Leaders in the Times of Jesus Christ The Teachings of Jesus Christ and Coins The Jewish War Judea Capta Bar Kockhba War Aelia Capitolina	32
8	Times of the Gentiles: 132 AD to 1914(17) AD	78
9	Times of the Gentiles: 1914(17) AD to 1947/48 AD; The Jews Return to the Land	88
10	History of the Jews 1947/48 - Current	96
11	Jewish Population and Timeline of Their History	108
12	Modern Jewish Coinage and Medals	110
13	Jews in the Land in the Last Days	116
14	Conclusions	117
	Bibliography	119
	Appendices Cut Coin Fractions, True False Religion Reflected in Coins, Ancient Coin Identification: Roman, Greek, and Jewish, Definitions of Ancient Prutah and Lepta, Use of Coins in Archaeology (Example: Bethsaida, Masada Fortress, and Ancient Jewish Sewage System), Ancient Coin Mints in Israel, Roman Noah's Ark Coin, Ptolemy Coin Hoard, Who Were the Magi, Who Were the Samarians and Samaritans, True and False Religions Portrayed in Coins, True and False Religions continued: the Orphic Stone vs. a Holy God, Smelting Metal and Examples of Raw Metals, Electrum, Clay Forger's Molds, Scripture relating to the Messiah, He is Risen	121
	What Must I Do to Know Jesus Christ?	154
	About the Author	155

Dr. John G. Leslie

Silver cast token made and given  to me by my daughter Anna

ACKNOWLEDGMENTS

Most photographs are taken by myself except for those noted in the footnotes, captions, or below. All rights are retained.

A. Permission for use of coin images is greatly appreciated from the following groups:

1) Robert Deutsch Archaeological Center for use of the Judea Capta coin of Vespasian. http://www.archaeological-center.com

2) Jethro from artancient.com for use of the Jewish War Year One sela, and the Bar Kochba coin Year Three with the Temple image. http://www.artancient.com

3) Joe Sermarini from Forum Ancient Coins for use of coin of Herod Agrippa 1 sacrificing a pig. http://www.forumancientcoins.com

4) D.S. Green for use of YHD Ptolemy coin (see dsgreen64 on Ebay for his coin sales).

5) Classic Numismatic Group for use of Roman Gordian III coin of Noah. http://www.cngcoins.com

6) David Hendin from Amphora Coins for the Year One Bar Kochba bronze coin. http://www.davidhendin.blogspot.com

B. Permission for use of Roman coin die image is greatly appreciated from the following group:

7) Lorenzo Moretti from Artemide Aste s.r.l. for the use of the Caesar Domitian iron coin die. http://www.deamoneta.com

C. Permission for use of pre-coin barter image is greatly appreciated from the following group:

8) David Hendin from Amphora Coins for the Hacksilber silver and bronze rings. http://www.davidhendin.blogspot.com

Cover: Coins representing the progression of history. From upper left to lower right: Electrum coin (earliest type of coin- Ionia), Persian Siglos with warrior and bow, Greek bronze image of Antiochus IV, Jewish bronze Hasmonean Hyrcanus 1 anchor, Roman bronze memorial image of Caesar Augustus, Tyre silver with image of the god Melkart, Jewish bronze First Jewish War Omer Cup, Jewish bronze Bar Kockhba War palm tree, Byzantine bronze with image of conqueror Constantine dragging prisoner, Crusader bronze with image of cross time of Hethoum, Ottoman silver, Jewish bronze Haganah Defense token, Jewish modern Israeli coin, Israeli token with Israel being replanted, European Union copper coin with image of a magician. (See text for the reading of inscriptions.)

Appreciation given to Jim Brown for review of the text and Barbara Leslie for editing it.

Dr. John G. Leslie

CHAPTER 1   INTRODUCTION

One might ask - why study coins? Because coins are a thumb print of given times in history and the Bible is replete with stories and the relevance of coins to the lives of different people in different places and times. Coins are a small archaeological gallery of ancient civilizations as well as current ones. Through coins and their uses we can understand something of the culture of a given society, the buying and selling of things, and the political aspirations of their leaders. They can be used to identify certain archaeological sites and these can then be correlated with other ones to gain a broader understanding of the inter-relationships of various societies.

Historical writings can be correlated as well. Coins give a glimpse into the religious beliefs of different cultures. This information can be utilized by Christian and Jewish peoples to better understand the temptations and deceptions wielded against their forbearers, and hopefully help them to become more wise and discerning.

Coins, in this text, will be used to help document much of Jewish history and its importance to God's plan for the peoples of the world. From the middle of Chapter 7 through Chapter 13 the history of Israel that is covered is not commonly considered "Biblical history", i.e. you can't look up chapter and verse in the Bible that takes place at the same time as these historical events. However, these years are more like an interim time period until more of Daniel's prophecies comes to pass (from Daniel 2:26-45, and Daniel chapters 7-12).

CHAPTER 2 HISTORY OF BARTER BEFORE COINAGE IN THE MIDDLE EAST

The earliest civilizations, post Flood, such as Akkad, Babylon and others (in Mesopotamia, now modern Iraq) were well-developed social caste systems with complex religious practices and commerce. Yet, stamped money as a barter unit was apparently not used. It was not devised, at least from archaeological evidence, till approximately 700-600 BC in the area of Lydia (Turkey). Prior to this time weights of rare metals (gold, silver, and copper) along with emblems of barter such as shells, bronze rings, and arrowhead weights were traded items (See **Figure: Emblems of Barter**) of exchange. Other items of exchange included cows or other livestock. The difficulty of portability and preservation of substances such as cattle necessitated an acceptable unit of barter. Lumps of rare metals became commonly used, but the lack of standard units and purity of the lumps required scales for every transaction. Because shell and bronze rings were easily counterfeited, these soon grew out of favor. By developing stamped coinage the Lydian bureaucracy defined and established specific units of barter and declared their authority over economic transactions in the areas where the coins were used. This concept rapidly spread to other areas including Greece and then to the Persian Empire. China, however, was casting precious metal in the forms of barter at an even earlier time than Lydia, but it would not develop uniform coinage as such till 680 AD. Even then it would cast and not stamp coins.[1] The use of barter and weights prior to coinage is acknowledged in the Bible. Hendin notes "There were no coins in ancient Israel during the days of the First Temple (960-586 BCE)…Before coins were invented barter was the method of trade."[2] He quotes Gen. 47:19, "Buy us and our land for food, and we and our land will be slaves to Pharaoh." He also quotes the Bible as referring to having "You shall have just balances, just weights, a just ephah (a unit of dry measure), and a just hin (a unit of liquid measure)."[3] A weight of silver is mentioned as early as Genesis 20:16.[4]

---

[1] "**Ancient Chinese Coinage** includes some of the earliest known coins. These coins, used as early as the Spring and Autumn period (770-476 BC), took the form of imitations of the cowrie shells that were used in ceremonial exchanges. The Spring and Autumn period also saw the introduction of the first metal coins; however, they were not initially round, instead being either knife shaped or spade shaped. Round metal coins with a round, and then later square hole in the center were first introduced around 350 BC…Ancient Chinese coins are markedly different from coins produced in the west. Chinese coins were manufactured by being cast in molds…" From: Wikipedia Ancient Chinese Coinage 2-8-14.

[2] Hendin, pg 25.

[3] Hendin, pg 27 (Leviticus 19:36).

[4] Gen. 20:16 "To Sarah he said, "Behold, I have given your brother a thousand pieces of silver; behold, it is your vindication before all who are with you, and before all men you are cleared." NIDOTTE: כֶּסֶף (kesep), silver, money **ANE** The Akk. *kaspu* appears to have originally been an adj. of the metal refined, indicated by some texts that use the word כֶּסֶף (a form of the word refine) for silver; eventually it completely repressed the original nom. The nom. is common both as a metal and a medium of exchange, even for other metals. It is found in Ugaritic and Phoenician as well as ancient Hebrew and Aramaic.

Emblems of Barter

Shell

Cast Bronze Ring

Cast Bronze Arrowhead

Cast Bronze Fish

Scales and Weights similar to Ancient Ones

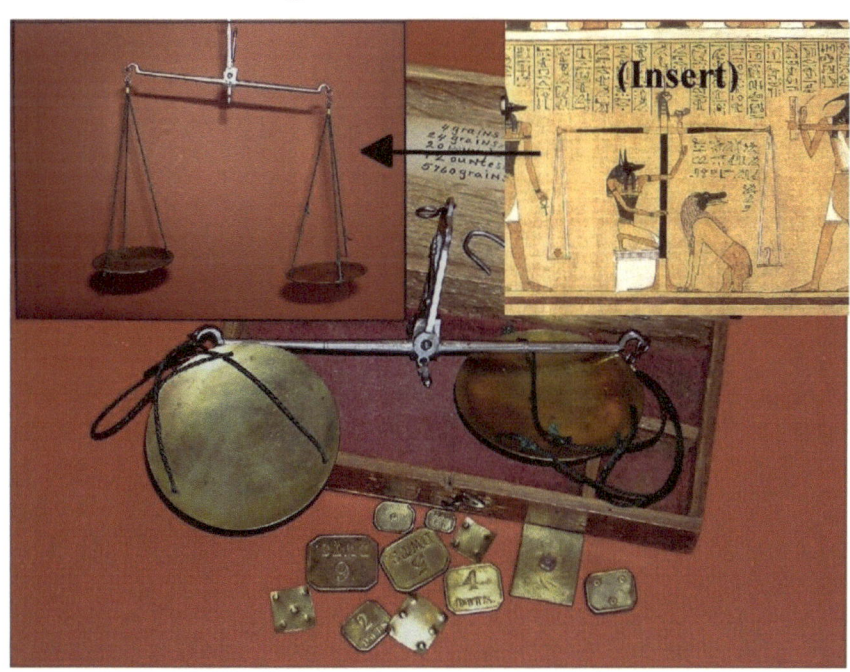

(Egyptian Panel: Scales From Book Of The Dead)

(public domain wikipedia 2-2015)

Jewish Pre-Coinage Commerce

Hacksilber silver ingot: "c. 8-6 centuries BC, cut silver ingot of 8.8 x 10mm, 1.12 grams. These are quite rare. Similar ingots were found at Ein Gedi in a terra cotta cookingpot, hidden in a building destroyed near the end of Iron Age II, early 6th century BC. Avi-Yonah Encylcopedia of the Holy Land, volume 2, p. 374.14."[5]

Bronze ring: "This is an Israelite Period (Iron Age c. 8th century BC) bronze bracelet-shaped currency ingot, around 9 cm diameter and weighs 140 grams, a bit heavier than the 'standard' type of 110-120 grams. (These are not denominational as currency, however they were traded by weight, and one can imagine that larger and smaller sizes were used.) These are often mistakenly believed to be bracelets, an idea which is quickly dissuaded by inability to slip in even a small hand, combined with the heavy weight, although one cannot rule out the possibility that they were also used as jewelry of some form."[6]

"Brody and Friedman note that 'bronze bracelets, anklets, circlets, rings, and rods may have served as a medium of exchange, each carrying a different monetary value...The use of bronze as an item of value--whether for status, prestige, or wealth--is well documented across the ancient world. The metal was strong, durable, had good color and shine...' --Brody, A. & Friedman, E. 'Bronze Bangles from Tell en-Nasbeh: Cultural and Economic Observations on an Artifact Type from the Time of the Prophets,' in Robert B. Coote and Norman K. Gottwarld, eds., To Break Every Yoke: Essays in Honor of Marvin L. Chaney. The Social World of Biblical Antiquity, Second Series, 3; Sheffield: Sheffield Phoenix Press, pp. 97-114."[7]

---

[5] D. Hendin online http://www.ebay.com/usr/amphoracoins. 6-4-2016. Photo permission D. Hendin.
[6] Ancient Scale Weights and Pre-Coinage Currency 4. Reference: Ancient Scale Weights and Pre-Coinage Currency 4.
[7] D. Hendin online http://ebay.com/usr/amphoracoins, 6-4-2016.

Jewish Pre-Coinage (600-800 BC)

Hacksilber silver ingot: Photo permit from D Hendin. Size not to scale.

Bronze rings: (6cm/33.8 gms and 9 cm/140 gms)

CHAPTER 3 DEVELOPMENT OF COIN STAMPING IN THE MIDDLE EAST: REVIEW OF HISTORY OF THE REGION

The coin stamping process that developed in Lydia[8] (700 BC) involved three steps:

1) On the end of a 5-6 inch bronze shaft (die) a flat engraving called an intaglio would be carved. On another flat block of bronze an engraving would be etched. 2) A coin planchette (blank), usually cast of a softer metal i.e. gold, silver, or copper would then be heated and placed on the top of the block engraving which had been placed in an anvil. 3) The engraved shaft, punch, was then placed on top of the planchette and struck with a mallet. The result was a coin with an engraved print on one side and the punch imprint or incuse on the opposite. (See **Figure: Method of Coin Stamping**) Rapid advances resulted with engravings being developed for both sides and with increased sophistication the entire surface of the coin was stamped uniformly.

The city states of Greece during the fourth-fifth century BC produced some of the most artistic coins in history. The obverse (front) side often showed leaders with flowing hair and graceful animals. The Persians who followed, in contrast produced simple stilted images reflective of a more staid culture. The first coins stamped in Jerusalem (YHD)[9] would be under Persian authority in the early fourth century BC. Greek coins were then infiltrated into the area following Alexander the Great's conquests in the late 4th century BC. After him the Romans produced many with political messages-military victories, economic contracts, or descriptive accolades of the Roman leader(s). Few had any artistic beauty (See **Appendix Figure on Coin Identification**). Throughout the several hundred years of the Roman Empire attempts were made to unify coinage amongst the vast areas, including the use of local mints to stamp coins with distinctive local characteristics. The Roman procurators and designated Kings of Judea would produce coins that date the times of Christ. The Jewish population rebelled against Roman authority (which had been harsh) in 66-74 AD and 132-135 AD. After much bloodshed on both sides the first rebellion, The Jewish War, was crushed. Coins with "Judea Capta" appeared reflecting Rome's success against the Jews. When the second rebellion, **Bar Kochba**, failed Rome then began to stamp coins in Jerusalem (renamed **Aelia Capitolina**) with the images of the Caesars and foreign gods like Tychae- which were offensive to the Jewish people who had been dispelled from the city.

---

[8] Sear, D.R. Greek Coins, vol. 2 Asia and Africa 1979, pg. xi. Also see Addendum on Electrum coins.
[9] "The **Yehud coinage** is a series of small silver coins bearing the Aramaic inscription *Yehud*. They derive their name from the inscription YHD, 'Yehud', the Aramaic name of the Achaemenid Persian province of Yehud; others are inscribed YHDH, the same name in Hebrew…The YHD coins are believed to date from the Persian period. On the other hand, it is possible that the YHDH coins are from the following Ptolemaic period." Wikipedia 11-15-15 and are referred to in Rooke, Deborah W., "Zadok's heirs: the role and development of the High Priesthood in ancient Israel" (Oxford, 2000) p.225.

Method of Coin Stamping

Cast Blank

Coin Die of Domitian (51-96 AD)

Permit:https://www.deamoneta.com/auctions/view/261/201

Provinance: Artemide Aste s.r.l.

Over the next 200 hundred years Christianity impacted the Roman culture at least politically. Religious motifs were developed on Roman coins reflecting Constantine's acceptance and subsequent proclamation of Christianity during the early decades of the third century AD. This became more pronounced as the Roman Empire transitioned into the Byzantine Period around 500 AD. (**See Figure: Byzantine Empire**.) Most coins of this period had images of Jesus Christ with the Apostles on the obverse and declarations such as "King of Kings, Lord of Lords" were written on the reverse.[10] Cup coins stamped in bronze are a unique coin type of this period.

The Islamic religion and political system which originated with Mohammed who was born 570 AD in what is now Saudi Arabia, would contest with the Byzantine Empire for hundreds of years. Eventually it overcame much of the Byzantine Empire and in 636 AD took Jerusalem. Its coinage would reflect this.[11] The Crusades would attempt to wrest the land back, but ultimately failed.[12] The Ottoman Empire, rulers from Turkey, would overtake other Arab leaders in approximately 1400 AD. They developed a unified empire until the end of World War One. (**See Figure: Ottoman Empire**.) The Ottomans exacted tribute from both Arab and Jew in conquered areas and little was done to improve the economic situation of those they ruled. Coins of this group often bear the image of the leader.

The Ottoman Empire came to an end at the conclusion of World War One. They had sided with Germany who had lost the war. England was given a mandate over the Middle East area. In the Balfour Declaration of 1917 the land of Israel[13] and the return of the Jewish people to their land was acknowledged; although Israel did not become a legitimate and separate nation until 1948. During the period of 1917 to 1948 the area of Palestine[14] (a Roman designation for the area) including Israel was under the Palestinian Authority, overseen by the English government. Coinage would reflect their authority in the area having the inscriptions of three languages: English, Arabic, and Hebrew. Once Israel became a nation in 1948 it began to produce its own coinage and still has three languages minted on the coinage.

---

[10] "Early Byzantine coins continue the late Roman conventions: on the obverse the head of the Emperor, now full face rather than in profile, and on the reverse, usually a Christian symbol such as the cross, or a Victory or an angel (the two tending to merge into one another)." Wikipedia Byzantine Coinage. 5-2015.

[11] Catalogue of the Imperial Byzantine Coins in the British Museum by William Wroth,1908.

[12] The area around Jerusalem would be contested for during the 'Middle Ages" as European kings would temporarily wrest it back from Islamic rule. This was ongoing from about 1071-1453 AD.

[13] "The **Land of Israel** (Hebrew: אֶרֶץ יִשְׂרָאֵל *'Ereṣ Yiśrā'ēl*, *Eretz Yisrael*) is one of several names for an area of indefinite geographical extension in the Southern Levant. Related biblical, religious and historical English terms include the Land of Canaan, the Promised Land, the Holy Land, and Palestine." fr Wikipedia 5-2015.

[14] "Palestine (Arabic: فلسطين *Filasṭīn, Falasṭīn, Filisṭīn*; Greek: Παλαιστίνη, *Palaistinē*; Latin: *Palaestina*; Hebrew: פלשתינה *Palestina*) is a geographic region in Western Asia between the Mediterranean Sea and the Jordan River. It is sometimes considered to include adjoining territories. The name was used by Ancient Greek writers, and was later used for the Roman province Syria Palaestina, the Byzantine Palaestina Prima and the Umayyad and Abbasid province of Jund Filastin." From Wikipedia online10-11-2014.

(Maps Public Domain)

CHAPTER 4 DANIEL'S DREAM: DIVISION OF MANKIND IN RELATIONSHIP TO THE JEWISH PEOPLE AND THE MERNEPTAH STELE

While secular histories of the earth diminish the significance of the Jewish people and the nation of Israel, in the council of God all of history revolves around it. This is because the Jews are God's witnesses to the other nations of the earth regarding God's sovereign rules, His faithfulness, and His dealings with mankind. When Judea or the southern kingdom[15] began to be taken into captivity to Babylon in 605 BC (Jerusalem being captured and destroyed in 587 BC) a young prince named Daniel was included. During his stay there he interpreted several dreams and one in particular of the king Nebuchadnezzar which outlined the rest of human history from that time forth. This dream is the format around which coins of Judea and the surrounding nations will be discussed.

The dream focused on the nations immediately in contact with Israel, and covers from the time of the neo-Babylonian Empire, 608-539 BC[2], to the end of the current age. It is still coming to pass, and is not affected by the perturbations in the nations of the earth, but does affect them. This will become fully manifest at the time of Armageddon when all the nations of the earth will be gathered against Israel on the mountains of that land. The dream, found in Daniel 2:36-45, placed Nebuchadnezzar King of Babylon as the head of gold followed by less consolidated kingdoms: Media-Persia as represented by arms and a chest of silver, Greece being represented by hips of bronze, and the Roman Empire as two long legs with toes of clay and iron. The legs represented the two parts of the empire. Physically/historically this has occurred and is continuing even to this day.

These kingdoms reflect the attempt by humans to rule by their own power and exalt themselves against God and the people He has chosen--the Jewish Race (descendants of Abraham, Isaac, and Jacob). God has allowed this to happen. But He demonstrated the faithfulness of His promise to the Jewish people that even when they sinned and He needed to chasten them, that He would never forsake them as a nation. He has consistently delivered them from other nations and brings glory to Himself in doing so.[16]

---

[15] The term "Jew" comes from the word "Judah," in Hebrew it is actually the same word. First given to one belonging to the tribe of Judah or to the separate kingdom of Judah (2 Kings 16:6; 25:25; Jer. 32:12; 38:19; 40:11; 41:3), in contradistinction from those belonging to the kingdom of the ten tribes, who were called Israelites. The name "Jew" is primarily tribal (from Judah). It is first found in 2 Kings 16:6, as distinct from Israel or Ephraim, of the northern kingdom. The usage of the word "Jew" in the Bible seems to have been applied after the captivity from Babylon; Israelites were called Jews to distinguish their ethnicity from Gentiles. During the Captivity, and after the Restoration, the name, was extended to the entire Hebrew nation without distinction (Esther 3:6, 10; Dan. 3:8, 12; Ezra 4:12; 5:1, 5). Originally this people were called Hebrews (Gen. 39:14; 40:15; Ex. 2:7; 3: 18; 5:3; 1 Sam. 4:6, 9, etc.), but after the Exile this name fell into disuse. From: http://www.letusreason.org/Biblexp265.htm. Please note that the tribe of Benjamin is/was associated with the tribe of Judah.

[16] It is important to note that while God deals with nations He also deals in a similar fashion with individuals.

Daniel's Seventy Weeks

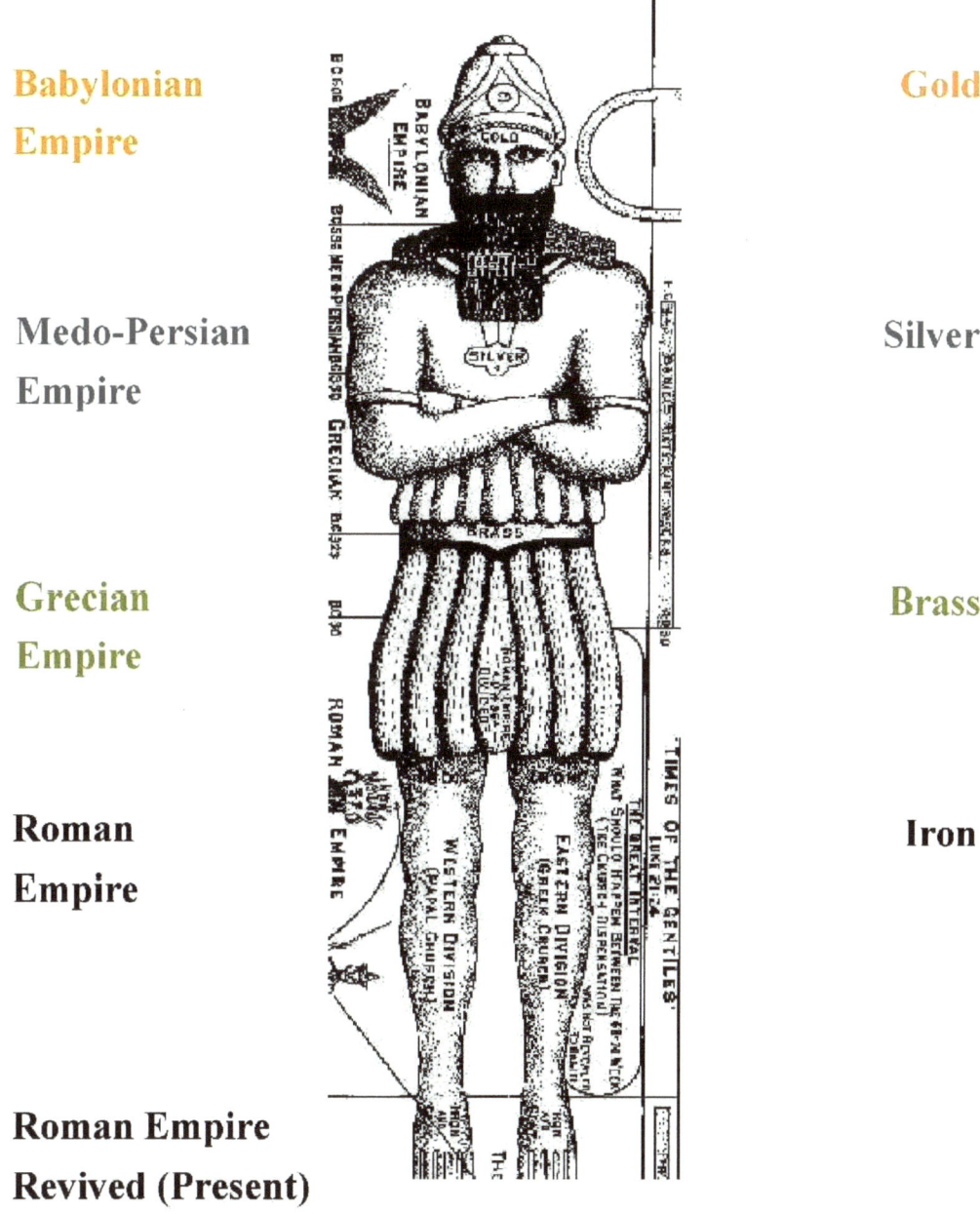

Babylonian Empire — Gold

Medo-Persian Empire — Silver

Grecian Empire — Brass

Roman Empire — **Iron**

Roman Empire Revived (Present)

From: C. Larkin *Dispensational Truth* 1918 Public Domain

The "children of Israel"[17] found themselves progressively, from 607 BC, in bondage to Nebuchadnezzar because of their sins. It was proclaimed by Jeremiah the Prophet this bondage would last 70 years (book of Jeremiah 25:11) because they did not practice tithing, nor the Year of Jubilee, and because of false sacrifices. They would begin to return to their land, Israel, in 537 BC. Later they would be sent into a second captivity (Diaspora) for rejecting the Messiah (the Christian view) or the Rebellion against Rome (the Jewish view). This would be culminated in the destruction of the Temple for a second time in 70 AD. Yet God would not abandon them but would eventually begin returning them back into the land in the latter days (as promised in the books of Ezekiel, Isaiah, Zechariah and others).[18]

The Dream also showed that the ascendency of each of man's kingdoms would not prevail. None did, though each had been used, and will be used to purify the Jewish people and to judge the unbelief of the other nations, races, and tribes of people. Even at this moment the revival of the Roman Empire as represented in the European Union is a tool by which God will purify His people. It is God's plan to return them to Himself. It is important that Christians remember that they are the Bride of Christ[19], but God the Father is the husband to the Jewish people.[20] They, the Jewish people and to some degree Christians, will be surrounded with increasing hatred and persecution by those who hate God, yet God will preserve them, though some will die (not fighting back) as martyrs. God has always shown Himself to be their protector. The Bible states, and history has shown, that God has always preserved a remnant of His people. In the book of Daniel the 10th chapter it says that a stone made without hands will crush

---

[17] The **Israelites** were a Semitic people of the Ancient Near East, who inhabited part of Canaan during the tribal and monarchic periods (15th to 6th centuries BCE), and lived in the region in smaller numbers after the fall of the monarchy. The term "Israelites" is the English term (derived from the ancient Greek) for the Hebrew biblical term *Bnei Yisrael* which properly translates as either "Sons of Israel" or "Children of Israel", and refers both to the direct descendants of the patriarch Jacob as well as the historical populations of the United Kingdom of Israel and Judah. In the post-exilic period, beginning in the 5th century BCE, the two known remnants of the Israelite tribes came to be referred to as Jews and Samaritans, inhabiting the territories of Judea, Galilee and Samaria. Other terms sometimes used include the "Hebrews" and the "Twelve Tribes" (of Israel). From: Wikipedia online 10-11-2014.

[18] "The former BBC Middle East correspondent, Tim Llewellyn, looks back at the history of Israel. The state of Israel was proclaimed by the Jewish leader, David Ben Gurion, on May 14, 1948, and officially came into being on the 15th, after British Mandatory rule ended at midnight. In many minds, the birth of Israel is closely identified with the Nazi terror in Europe and the Holocaust, but in fact the conception of and planning for a Jewish state had begun some 60 years earlier." From: http://news.bbc.co.uk/2/hi/events/israel_at_50/history/78597.stm

[19] "The imagery and symbolism of marriage is applied to Christ and the body of believers known as the church. These are those who have trusted in Jesus Christ as their personal savior and have received eternal life. In the New Testament, Christ, the Bridegroom, has sacrificially and lovingly chosen the church to be His bride (Ephesians 5:25-27). Just as there was a betrothal period in biblical times during which the bride and groom were separated until the wedding, so is the bride of Christ separate from her Bridegroom during the church age. Her responsibility during the betrothal period is to be faithful to Him (2 Corinthians 11:2;Ephesians 5:24). At the Second Coming of Christ, the church will be united with the Bridegroom, the official "wedding ceremony" will take place and, with it, the eternal union of Christ and His bride will be actualized (Revelation 19:7-9;21:1-2)." Read more:http://www.gotquestions.org/bride-of-Christ.html#ixzz3Fwnf0Izp

[20] "God explicitly declares Himself to be Israel's Husband in several places in the Prophets. Isaiah penned, "For your Maker is your husband — the LORD Almighty is his name — the Holy One of Israel is your Redeemer; he is called the God of all the earth." (Isa 54:5, NIV) Jeremiah also points to the Lord as Israel's Husband in the following, ""Return, faithless people," declares the LORD, "for I am your husband." (Jeremiah 3:14, NIV) These references clearly show that the Lord Almighty considered Himself to be Israel's "Husband." The Prophets also speak of Israel as God's Bride and the Lord as Israel's Bridegroom. "As a young man marries a maiden, so will your sons marry you; as a bridegroom rejoices over his bride, so will your God rejoice over you." (Isa 62:5, NIV) "'I remember the devotion of your youth, how as a bride you loved me and followed me through the desert, through a land not sown." (Jer 2:2b, NIV) This tender language is meant to give Israel, and mankind by extension, a clear perspective on how the Lord views His personal relationship with them." From: http://www.wholeword.net/wp-content/uploads/2012/03/The-Bride-In-The-Old-Testament.pdf

Daniel's Seventy Weeks In Coins

Babylon (Ionia coin)	Persian	Greek	Roman	Revived Roman
600 BC		Time (Approximately)		Present 2000 AD

Rome and Israel Through Time

Caesar Augustus   Ancient Rome   **Anti-Christ   Revived Rome**

Hasmonian   Ancient   Israel   **Modern   Israel**

Judea Capta   **Judea Liberata**

(coin photo permit Robert Deutsch)   (Coins not comparative in scale)   (Commemorative medal)

100 BC-135 AD   Time (Approximately)   **Present 2000 AD**

those who oppose Him. And in that day the remnant of Jewish people will look upon and see Him whom they have pierced and weep. A fountain will be opened to the house of David (Zechariah 12:10-14). At that time, called the End of the Age, Israel becomes the head and not the tail of the nations. And Jesus Christ will rule from Jerusalem for a thousand years (the Millennium). After this comes the "New Heavens and New Earth".[21]

Coins are actual physical evidence of these events. The Babylonians used weights of raw metals and shell rings for trade, but the Persians began to stamp the precious metals with their images and developed a uniform coinage system.[22] The gold **Daric**, and the silver **Siglos** of Darius (as mentioned in Daniel 5:31) were of a known given weight and signified a certain purchasing power.

The spread of the Greek Empire has been confirmed in the distribution of coins dropped, or used in the trade/sale of items. Often the profiles of Greek gods, for example Zeus, and great kings were represented on these coins. The engraving was in the Greek language. In areas where Alexander the Great conquered he brought this monetary system and required a unified coinage system for trade.

Rome further consolidated a monetary system allowing local regional control regarding the design of the edifices on them. Local people groups were allowed to exalt their gods as well as the Roman pantheon of gods. Victories and treaties and the name of the Caesar or Emperor were displayed on the coins as well.

In the reunification of the modern European currency (unit Euro) we see the most viable evidence of the re-consolidation of the old Roman Empire. Yet, its unity is less in that it is an amalgam of iron and clay- weak and strong nations not mixing well together. It may be that this will mark or lead to the advent of a rise to power of the man described in the book of Daniel as the Antichrist. Yet, Daniel further describes the return of the Messiah as a stone cut without human hands who will crush this self exalted human leader.

French 2 Cent (2000): Obverse, Image of Marianne, national symbol of the French Republican, symbol of the allegory of liberty and reason, and a portrayal of the "Goddess of Liberty".[23] Reverse side has a picture of the earth with the Europe/Africa/Middle East/Western Asia side of the globe seen with 12 stars surrounding it. It is copper plated steel, 1.67 cm, 3.06 gm.[24] The face on the front clearly has a mystical spiritualist appearance, the "Goddess of Liberty". It reflects the spiritism now present in Europe. (In the map on the opposite page of the European Union countries, it should be noted that the United Kingdom (England) has been a part of the EU, but has currently stepped out of membership.)

---

[21] There are many books on these subjects, with some varying of how the details will work out. I like Clarence Larkin. See online: http://www.preservedwords.com/disptruth/title.htm;
[22] Achaemid coinage was introduced about 520-480 BC. Initially a Siglos weighed between 10.73-10.92 gm and was 97-98% silver. The gold Daric was 8.10-8.50 gm and 98-99% pure. 20 Siglos =1 Daric. Siglos in picture dated 475-420 B.C. Information from: Wikipedia online 5-2015.
[23] https://en.wikipedia.org/wiki/Marianne
[24] https://www.fleur-de-coin.com/coin-shop/France-2-cents-2000-Depicts-young-feminine-Marianne_eur1226

European Union Countries
(Most Countries)

(Map Wikipedia Public Domain 6-16-16 labels added)

The Merneptah Stele

"The Merneptah Stele has long been touted as the earliest extra biblical reference to Israel. The ancient Egyptian inscription dates to about 1205 BCE and recounts the military conquests of the pharaoh Merneptah. Near the bottom of the hieroglyphic inscription, a people called "Israel" is said to have been wiped out by the conquering pharaoh. This has been used by some experts as evidence of the ethno genesis of Israel around that time." [25]

"The **Merneptah Stele**—also known as the **Israel Stele** or **Victory Stele of Merneptah** is an inscription by the Ancient Egyptian king Merneptah (reign: 1213 to 1203 BC) discovered by Flinders Petrie in 1896 at Thebes, and now housed in the Egyptian Museum in Cairo. The text is largely an account of Merneptah's victory over the Libyans and their allies, but the last 3 of the 28 lines deal with a separate campaign in Canaan, then part of Egypt's imperial possessions. While alternative translations have been put forward, the majority of biblical archeologists translate a set of hieroglyphs on Line 27 as "Israel", such that it represents the first documented instance of the name Israel in the historical record, and the only mention in Ancient Egypt. It is also one of only four known ancient inscriptions interpreted to mention the term "Israel", the others being the Mesha Stele, the Tel Dan Stele, and the Kurkh Monolith. As a result, some consider the stele to be Flinders Petrie's most famous discovery, an opinion with which Petrie himself concurred." [26]

---

[25] The author also notes another possible inscription dated to 1400 BC with the name Israel: "Manfred Görg discovered a broken statue pedestal containing hieroglyphic name-rings in the Egyptian Museum of Berlin and, after studying it with colleagues Peter van der Veen and Christoffer Theis, suggest that one of the name-rings should be read as "Israel." Not all scholars agree with their reading because of slight differences in spelling." http://www.biblicalarchaeology.org/daily/ancient-cultures/ancient-israel/does-the-merneptah-stele-contain-the-first-mention-of-israel/

[26] Wikipedia on the Merneptah Stele online 10-30-15.

Merneptah Stele (1213-1203 BC)

Early Mention of Name Israel

Line 27 reads "the people of **Israel** is laid waste-their crops are not"

Lithograph F.Petrie 1800's Photo
Public Domain Wikipedia 1-4-14

CHAPTER 5   TIMES OF THE JEWS UPON RETURN FROM BABYLON DURING THE PERSIAN PERIOD AND TRANSITION TO THE GREEK PERIOD

The Jewish people as groups began to return to the area of Israel after the 70 years of captivity in Babylon. Some initially followed Zerubbabel in 535 BC. They began to rebuild the Temple. Another group came with Nehemiah in 445 BC to restore the walls of Jerusalem. As a satrapy of Medo-Persia coins stamped in the area reflected the Persian King motif or were copies of coin produced by nearby Greek mints. Subsequent coinage reflected rule by Greek (Seleucid) and Egyptian (Ptolemy) rulers, and then briefly by Jewish leaders (Maccabean) till Roman rule prevailed.

Row 1) **Yehud**: These tiny silver coins were unique in that they identified the area of Judea with the archaic letters *Yhd* or *Yehud* (a derivative of Judea). In the photograph a U.S. quarter is used to demonstrate its size. Persian documents refer to the satrapy of Judea. They were produced about 400-300 BC. (A) Coin with falcon head left-reflecting the national symbol of Persia during the Achaemenid Dynasties (Cyrus the Great, Darius and others).[27] (B) The owl found on some coins is consistent with a Grecian motif. It is associated with Athena and represents wisdom and knowledge. This motif was carried into Roman religious beliefs.[28] This coin has the YHD in Hebrew on it. Both were minted before 333 BC.[29]

Row 2) **Alexander the Great:** Greek, tetradrachm: Obv. Bust of Herakles to right with lion skin covering his head and rev. Zeus seated on backless throne, eagle in right hand and scepter to the left. EI below throne =Sidon as mint. Torch below eagle. Inscription ALEXANDROU. Year of mint between 336-323 BC.[30]

Row 3) **Antiochus the 4th**: Obv. Radiate head to right, as Antiochus came to believe that he was a god; rev. "biga" fast two horse chariot. This reflected his aggressive campaigns. Mint probably Ptolemais in 174-164 BC.[31]

Row 4) **Antiochus VII/ John Hyracanus 1**: This particular coin, a prutah, is important as it reflects the transition from a complete Seleucid control of Israel to more autonomy by the Jewish leaders. On the obverse of this coin is the anchor a symbol of the Seleucids, and on the reverse the Lilly a symbol commonly found in Jewish art. The anchor derived from the birthmark of one of the Seleucid kings, and the Lilly has been found as a motif in the Temple. This coin was produced about 130-132 BC.[32]

---

[27] https://en.wikipedia.org/wiki/Emblem_of_Iran. See #429 in Hendin, 2001, pg. 90.
[28] https://en.wikipedia.org/wiki/Owl_of_Athena
[29] The early coins minted in Judea were patterned after ones stamped in Athens. D. Hendin Persian Silver of Judah www.anspocketchange.org/persian-silver-of-judah/
[30] https://www.brown.edu/Departments/Joukowsky_Institute/publications/papers /alexander_coinage
[31] http://www.wildwinds.com/coins/greece/seleucia/antiochos_IV/t.html
[32] Hendin 2001, #451, pg. 125-129.

Times of the Jewish People: Return From Babylon then Persian to Grecian to Hasmonean Rule of Judea

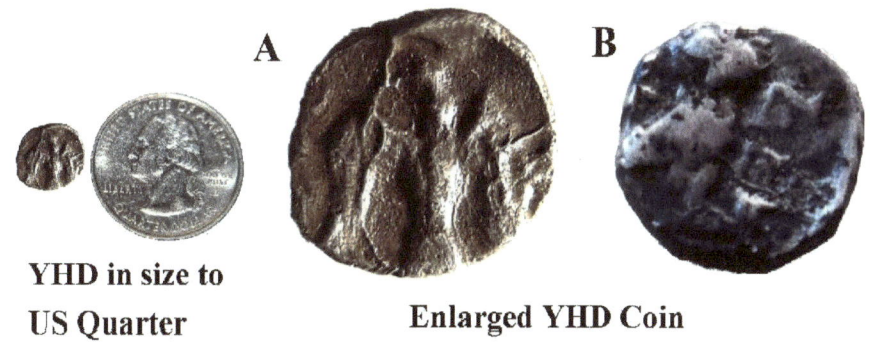

YHD in size to US Quarter   **Enlarged YHD Coin**

Persian Authority (above)

Alexander the Great

Antiochus IV "Epiphanes"

Antiochus VII/John Hyrcanus 1

Selucid (Greek) Authority (above)

(Coins not to comparative size-except YHD to US quarter.)

The Hezekiah Yehud Coin: Marker of Transition

There were coins produced in Judea at the end of the Persian rule that had the lettering in Aramaic of "Governor Hezekiah". This was not the well known Hezekiah of earlier Bible times but a later governor of Jerusalem. The progression of letterings from "Governor Hezekiah" to just "Hezekiah" to no mention of Hezekiah would mark the transition from Persian to Greek to Egyptian Ptolemaic rule in Judea.[33]

Coins, from a 1st period, about 340-336 BC, had the lettering "Governor (Hapach) Hezekiah (Yehezio)" along both sides of the owl.[34]

Coins from a 2nd group, about 336-302 BC, had only "Hezekiah".

With Alexander the Great's takeover of Judea in 332 BC the lettering was no longer placed on the new coins, but some production with lettering seems to have still continued at Acre, Sidon, Babylon and possibly Jerusalem (per the author of the article).[35]

Current coin displayed (Mid section): Is from a transition from the 1st to the 2nd Period as there are traces of lettering, "Hezekiah", on the left side and a branch on the right side of the owl. The Obv. is blank as is the case in many of these coins. Others, like the drawing at the top have a face, but it is uncertain of whom it portrayed. The image of the coin with the face had well worn lettering as well. The weight of the coin is 0.21 gm and diameter 7.3 mm.

Coins during the Ptolemaic era would take on a new design starting in 302 BC, with an image of Ptolemy on one side and an eagle with Aramaic writing for Judea on the other. See coin at bottom: Obv. Ptolemy 1 diademed bust right. Rev. Eagle, wings spread and standing left, with legend YHDH. Hendin #1087 ed. 2010. Weight 0.17 gm and diameter 6.5 mm. With photo permission from DS Green.

It should be noted that barter was still largely used during this time as well.

---

[33] Bar Kochba and J. Kindler reprint of Pseudo-Hecataeus on the Jews Legitimizing the Jewish Diaspora: Appendix A, 1997. University of California Press, pg. Summary and 256-270.

[34] Hendin stated "The first coins with Hebrew inscriptions were struck during the the period when the Achaemenid or Persian Empire ruled ancient Judah. It seems likely that the earliest of those coins were struck at the Philistian mint of Gaza between 539-333 BCE." D. Hendin *Persian Silver of Judah* on www.anspocketchange.org/persian-silver-of-judah/

[35] Ibid pg. 263.

The Hezekiah Yehud Coin: Marker of Transition

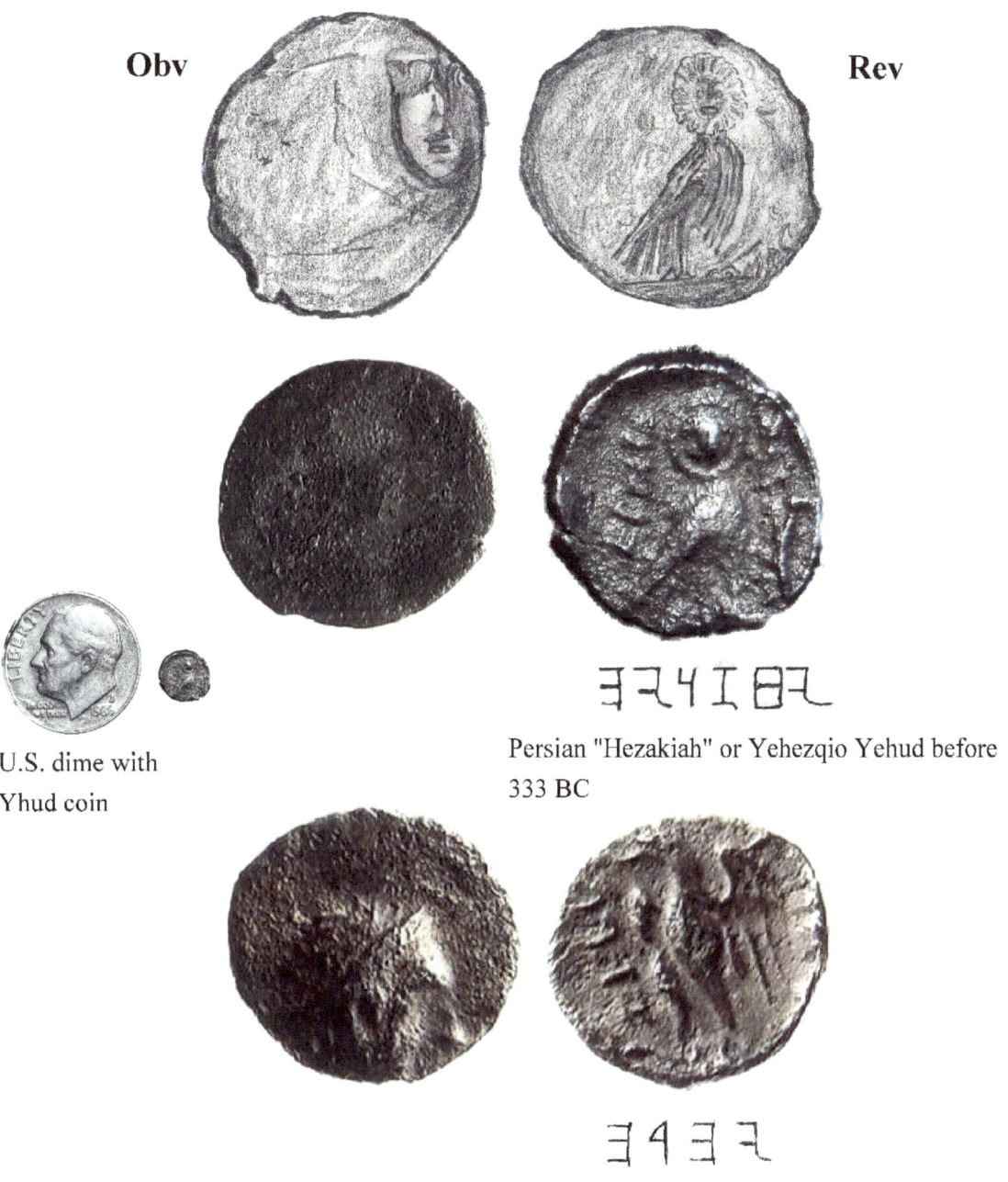

U.S. dime with Yhud coin

Persian "Hezakiah" or Yehezqio Yehud before 333 BC

Ptolemy "Governor" Yehud coin after 333 BC
Image from DS Green with Permit

CHAPTER 6   HISTORY OF THE HASMONEAN RISE TO POWER IN JUDEA

The Hasmonean Dynasty began with **Judah Maccabeus**[36] in a revolt against Greek rulers, Antiochus Epiphanes IV, in 167 BC and closed in 37 BC when it was replaced by the Herodian Dynasty. The Herods were put in place by Roman authorities.[37]

Judah, one of several sons of Mattathias (a Hasmonean), assisted his father in a revolt against Antiochus Epiphanes 4th. Antiochus had forbade the Jews from worshipping at the Temple in Jerusalem and had placed a statue of Jupiter above the altar. As well, pigs were to be slaughtered in various towns with Jews being required to attend. This offended the Jews. Grayzel describes the event:

"The '*Desolating abomination*'-To Antiochus the unwillingness of the Jews to be Hellenized was stiff-necked nonsense. If Judaism stood in his way, so much the worse for Judaism. He gave orders that Judaism must be destroyed. A part of the Syrian army marched into Jerusalem to support Menelaus[38]…many of the inhabitants of the city were killed…only the known Hellenists remained. Orders were given prohibiting the observance of the Sabbath, the holidays and circumcision. In the Temple above the altar was placed a statue of Jupiter bearing an obvious resemblance to Antiochus…To that statue were brought sacrifices the animal most detested by the Jews, the pig. An abominable act had been perpetrated on that 25th day of Kislev in the year 168 BC and, to use the descriptive expression of the Book of Maccabees, it left the Jewish people desolate…"[39]

In a little farming town northwest of Jerusalem, called Modin lived a man Mattathias from a priestly family of the *Hasmonaim*. He and his 5 sons were greatly grieved as they knew that soon the Syrians would require the sacrifice of a pig in their town. "The dreaded moment soon came…in the market place of the town…the Syrian soldiers erected an altar…A pig was produced which the soldiers had brought with them, and Mattathias, as priest and elder, was ordered to sacrifice it to Jupiter in honor of Antiochus. Mattathias did not move. From out of the crowd a young Jew stepped forward..a Hellenizer…he asked permission to perform the sacrifice…The apostate Jew approached the animal…Suddenly, in the twinkling of eye, the entire scene was transformed…The aged Mattathias, standing closest to the captain of the troops snatched the sword out of the captain's hand, and ran it through the body of the traitor."…Other Jews then grabbed weapons from the soldiers and killed them including the captain. Mattathias was then recorded to have said, "Whoever is for God, let him come unto me" and the successful revolt began.[40] (Grayzel, 1947, reprint 1949)

---

[36] Josephus Antiquities of the Jews Book 7:6 "when those that were appointed by the king were come to Modin, that they might compel the Jews to do what they were commanded, and to enjoin those that were there to offer sacrifice, as the king had commanded, they desired that Mattathias, a person of the greatest character among them, both on other accounts, and particularly on account of such a numerous and so deserving a family of children, would begin the sacrifice, because his fellow citizens would follow his example, and because such a procedure would make him honored by the king. But Mattathias said he would not do it; and that if all the other nations would obey the commands of Antiochus, either out of fear, or to please him, yet would not he nor his sons leave the religious worship of their country…"

[37] "The Hasmoneans" Wikipedia 5-14-15.

[38] A Jew and High Priest, not even of a priestly line, was an advocate of Hellenization.

[39] Ibid "The Hasmoneans" Wikipedia.

[40] Grayzel, pg 56-59.

INSERT

The Maccabean Revolt

Antiochus Epiphanes 4th

Coin with portrait of Antiochus IV. Reverse: Apollo seated on an omphalos. The Greek inscription reads ΒΑΣΙΛΕΩΣ ΑΝΤΙΟΧΟΥ ΘΕΟΥ ΕΠΙΦΑΝΟΥΣ ΝΙΚΗΦΟΡΟΥ (King Antiochus, the divine Epiphanus, Bringer of Victory. (From Wikipedia Public Domain).

Chapter 1: [20] In the year 143, after the conquest of Egypt, Antiochus marched with a great army against the land of Israel and the city of Jerusalem. [21] In his arrogance, he entered the Temple and took away the gold altar, the lampstand with all its equipment, [22] the table for the bread offered to the Lord, the cups and bowls, the gold fire pans, the curtain, and the crowns. He also stripped all the gold from the front of the Temple [23] and carried off the silver and gold and everything else of value, including all the treasures that he could find stored there. [24] Then he took it all to his own country. He had also murdered many people and boasted arrogantly about it. [25] There was great mourning everywhere in the land of Israel.. [29] Two years later Antiochus sent a large army from Mysia[d] against the towns of Judea. When the soldiers entered Jerusalem, [30] their commander spoke to the people, offering them terms of peace and completely deceiving them. Then he suddenly launched a fierce attack on the city, dealing it a major blow and killing many of the people. [31] He plundered the city, set it on fire, and tore down its buildings and walls. [32] He and his army took the women and children. [33] Then Antiochus and his forces built high walls and strong towers in the area north of the Temple, turning it into a fort.. [41-43] Antiochus now issued a decree that all nations in his empire should abandon their own customs and become one people. All the Gentiles and even many of the Israelites submitted to this decree. They adopted the official pagan religion, offered sacrifices to idols, and no longer observed the Sabbath.. [44] The king also sent messengers with a decree to Jerusalem and all the towns of Judea, ordering the people to follow customs that were foreign to the country. [45] He ordered them not to offer burnt offerings, grain offerings, or wine offerings in the Temple, and commanded them to treat Sabbaths and festivals as ordinary work days. [46] They were even ordered to defile the Temple and the holy things in it.[e] [47] They were commanded to build pagan altars, temples, and shrines, and to sacrifice pigs and other unclean animals there. [48] They were forbidden to circumcise their sons and were required to make themselves ritually unclean in every way they could, [49] so that they would forget the Law which the Lord had given through Moses and would disobey all its commands. [50] The penalty for disobeying the king's decree was death." 1 Maccabees 1:20-50 **Chapter 2:** [23] Just as he finished speaking, one of the men from Modein decided to obey the king's decree and stepped out in front of everyone to offer a pagan sacrifice on the altar that stood there. [24] When Mattathias saw him, he became angry enough to do what had to be done. Shaking with rage, he ran forward and killed the man right there on the altar. [25] He also killed the royal official who was forcing the people to sacrifice, and then he tore down the altar. [26] In this way Mattathias showed his deep devotion for the Law, just as Phinehas had done when he killed Zimri son of Salu. From: **1 Maccabees**

Mattathias soon died, and his son Judah took up the banner. He was to be called **Judah Maccabeus**.[41] They would carry on protracted guerrilla warfare against the Syrians (Greeks), until a certain battle, The Battle of Emmaus. The Maccabees destroyed much of the Syrian force in a night battle in the mountains. They recovered much "booty". From there they went to Jerusalem, cleansed the Temple including erecting a new altar. They re-established worship to God on the 25th of Kislev 165 BCE. A dedication feast called Hanukkah was performed for eight days. A miracle occurred as Grayzel recounts:

"The Talmud, for its part, relates the miracle of the little cruse containing enough oil to light the Temple menorah for only one day; this oil burned on for eight days, until the priests could prepare more oil untouched by pagan hands."[42]

Lysias, Antiochus' subordinate general, would return. He besieged Jerusalem. He offered terms in which "Syria would refrain from interfering in the internal conflicts between the Hasidim and the Hellenizing Jews…" Menelaus was executed. "…Judah and his fellow leaders would not be punished"….but the walls of Jerusalem would be razed, Syria would to continue to rule over Judea and continue to appoint the High Priest. The majority of Jews accepted this proposal. But the new High Priest, Alcimus, would violate every aspect of the treaty. The civil war renewed, but Judah Maccabeus would eventually die in battle not fully supported by the overall Jewish population.[43] (Yet, the Hasmoneans would remain in control of the Jews for about 100 years.)

Jonathan, Judah's younger brother, would succeed him in about 152 till 142 BC. Grayzel says that "one permanent result of the conflict was the unfading memory of Jewish heroism." He and the other Maccabees would finally gain peace with the Syrians, but the internal conflicts among the various groups of Jews vying for power would remain.[44] He gained favor with the Syrians and even became High Priest, governor, and a member of Syrian nobility. He would also court the Romans in a manner that would cause the Jewish people problems 100 years later.[45] In Grayzel's eyes Jonathan advanced political initiatives for the Jewish people, and maybe for himself; but Judah promoted religious ones.[46]

After the death of Jonathan at the hands of a "treacherous Syrian general", **Simon** an older brother, became the leader of the Jewish people. He was considered a "wise and calm man". Simon was appointed "Ruler and High Priest" by the Great Assembly.[47] Because of his age he did not go to battle, but left that to his sons. He died in 135 BC, and a son **John Hyrcanus I** would take control.

---

[41] There is some discussion why the surname of Maccabeus was taken, but possibly from *Makkebet* which means 'hammer'. Grayzel, pg. 59.
[42] Grayzel, pg. 63.
[43] Grayzel, pg. 64-65.
[44] Grayzel, pg. 65.
[45] Grayzel, pg. 70.
[46] Grayzel, pg. 71.
[47] Grayzel, pg.72- 73. "Such assemblies had been called on previous critical occasions, for example, to ratify the reforms of Ezra and Nehemiah…the aristocracy which had dominated previous assemblies had in the meantime become identified with the Hellenizing Jews, so that if they were represented at all, they were outvoted. The leaders of the Hasidic party were in the majority. The Sanhedrin of a later date claimed to have developed out of this assembly." Also, the religious leaders did not know who was from the Davidic line at that time so they elected Simon as "Ruler and High Priest…until a true prophet should arise."

John Hyrcanus I: The Syrian King Antiochus VII, with lessening influence in Judea, would offer Hyrcanus terms of peace with the following conditions: Hyrcanus would need to continue to consider himself a subject of Syria, all pagan cities except for the port of Jaffa must be returned. The influence of the Hellenizing Jews lessened with the decreasing influence of the Syrian government. In contrast, Hyrcanus began a policy of expansion. Grayzel has stated, "When nations start on the road of conquest they do not know where to stop. Between expansion for the sake of economic welfare and expansion for the sake of power and glory is but one short step." Idumæa was very important for trade routes between Egypt and Asia. "Hyrcanus used this as an excuse for conquering and annexing that entire country. More serious, in order to make sure of Idumea's loyalty, he actually compelled the Idumeans to adopt Judaism."[48] Grayzel then makes the note:

"Here was a grandson of Mattathias violating the very principle, religious freedom, which a previous generation had so nobly defended."[49]

Hyrcanus I would become known for his expansionist policies, and would draw various seekers of power to himself. In the Sanhedrin (the religious body) two groups arose: The Pharisees, or "separated ones" who opposed Hyrcanus's expansion policies on more on isolationist grounds; and the Sadducees who were more in favor of a strong nation accepted expansion. The Pharisees had a more "liberal" approach to the scriptures than the Sadducees.[50] Yet, the ordinary farmer or artisan, people that Hyrcanus's forbearers came from, would not support him; for they were the ones who had to send their sons to war and pay the taxes for it.

The sons, and subsequent leaders, having grown up in the circumstances of power seeking, intrigue, Hellenization, and a name of Judaism but not really a life of living it would become more and more secular in their worldview and actions.

Aristobulus I, ruler for only one year in 104-103 BC, was a lover of Greek things. His Jewish name was Judah but Greek was Aristobulus. Upon gaining power he threw three brothers in prison, and murdered a fourth one. He called himself king (*melech*) though he was not of the Davidic line. He died from drinking, disease, and a chronic fear of rebellion.[51]

Alexander Jannai, Aristobulus' only brother still alive, practiced the same policy as Aristobulus. He ruled for 22 years, 103-76 BC. Apparently a ruthless king, attempts were made to remove him from power by the Pharisees, but failed. When common people pelted him with citrons during Sukkot, he had the guards kill hundreds of them. When the advantage allowed, he had 800 Pharisees crucified at a garden party for the Sadducees. The separation between the two groups would not be repaired.[52]

Salome Alexandra, Jannai's wife, upon ascension in 76 BCE, restored the Pharisees and removed the Sadducees from the Sanhedrin.[53] She ruled, in relative peace, for 9 years 76-67 BC.

---

[48] Grayzel pg 74-75. The Herods would come from Idumea. This would have serious consequences for the Jewish people in Israel.
[49] Gryzel, pg. 75.
[50] Grayzel, pg.75- 77. The Sadducees supported forced conversion of the Idumeans.
[51] Grazel, pg. 79-80.
[52] Grazel, ptg. 80-81.
[53] Grayzel, pg. 82. The Council of State at that time had two roles: legislature and supreme court.

Sadly the Pharisees supported Jannai's son **John Hyrcanus II**, but he was not considered to have a strong personality to lead; and the Saduccees supported the younger son **Aristobulus II**, but he lacked wisdom and was ambitious.[54] As well, it is controversial as to whether Aristobulus II minted any coins during his brief rule.[55]

The two sons would vie for the throne, but Hyrcanus II's inability to lead initially caused him to default to the younger brother, Aristobulus II who subsequently ruled from 66-63 BC. Hyrcanus II would then rule from 63-40 BC. Aristobulus' son Alexander married Hyrcanus II's daughter Alexandra.

A clever Idumean, **Antipater**, would move into this relative vacuum of authority. He would make friends with Hyrcanus II. At the same time he had made connections with Pompey the Roman. He and Hyrcanus agreed to involve the Nabatean Arabs to attack Jerusalem and remove Aristobulus II. Pompey then contacted the Nabateans to remove their siege, which they did. An appeal was made to Rome by the two brothers and the Pharisees whom wanted constitutional control and the brothers out.

Aristobulus II after a siege of Jerusalem surrendered to the Romans, and gave it up. The Pharisees agreed to open the gates but the Sadducces did not. They, however, locked themselves in the Temple. When the Romans broke through into the Temple they slaughtered any in their path, even priests while some were performing a sacrifice.

One Hasmonean, **Mattathias Antigonus** (Aristobulus' youngest son) who had escaped to Parthia earlier, invaded Judea and came to the gates of Jerusalem. Through intrigue he lured Hyrcanus II to meet with him outside the city. There he cut off Hyrcanus's ear making him unable to be High Priest (no defect could be on the body of the High Priest). He ruled in Jerusalem for 2 years, from 40-37 BC, as a weak leader.

In conclusion, Hyrcanus II did not have the capability to lead, Aristobulus II was too ambitious, and the Pharisees were ignored. While Hyrcanus II was chosen and was a leader from 63-40 BC, and then lost his authority to Antigonus; it was really Antipater, the Idumean, a clever man with ties to Rome who was the leader in Judea. In a last act against the Hasmoneans he had Antigonus killed in 37 BC (with Rome's approval). The Maccabean (Hasmonean) Dynasty had come to an end.[56]

---

[54] Grayzel, pg. 82-83.
[55] Hendin, D. (2008) This coin expert feels that Aristobulus II may not have minted any coins as both he and Aristobulus I were named "Yehudah", and his reign was very short. Online: New Data Sheds Light on the Hasmonean Coin Theories. http://coinproject.com/jan/volume1/Issue1/volume1-1-3.html. From: The Journal of Ancient Numismatics 2008 vol. 1, issue1(April/May).
[56] Greyzel, pg. 91. It also appears that Antipater may have had Aristobulus II murdered. As well, he maneuvered through several political dangers such as backing Pompey rather the Julius Caesar, then he collected taxes for Brutus and Cassius when Anthony and Octavius came out victors. He survived both mistakes and was appointed to rule in Israel.

The Hasmoneans and Maccabeans

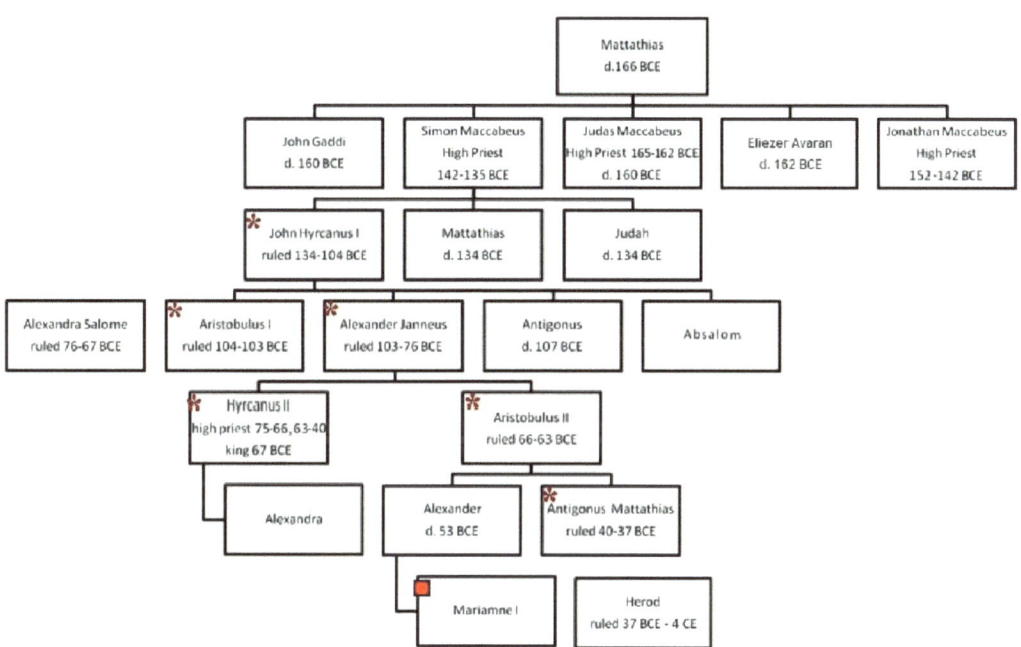

Permit CC BY-SA 3.0 from Marshall46 on Wikipedia 2-24-15

Asterix indicates rulers that minted coins-added by JGL

Square indicates that Mariamne 1 married Herod (the Great)-added by JGL

Hasmonean: may be derieved from Mattahia's family name of Hasmonai which has the connotation of being "princely" and possibly of a priestly origin. This caused some concern among Jews at the time as the Torah did not allow king and priest to be of the same lineage. Gen. 49:12 and Num. 3:6-9. **Maccabean**: may be derived from the aramaic term "makkaba" or hammer and was given to Judas for his fierce temper in battle. See myjewishlearning.com and Wikipedia on the Maccabeans.

Hasmonean Coins

Maccabean Coins: These coins were produced by several Hasmonean (Maccabean) leaders from about 167-38 BC in Israel, mostly in bronze. Most have on the one side "Yehohanan[57] the high priest and council of the Jews" or variations to this. The other side often has two cornucopias and a pomegranate reflecting prosperity (i.e. under their leadership). [58]These coins were in circulation during Christ's life, but stamping stopped with the control of the region by the Herods (of Idumean descent) and the Romans.

1) John Hyrcanus I/Antiochus VII: Obv. Anchor upsides down which reflects the Seleucid Kingdom and authority over Judea. It reads in Greek "King Antiochus benefactor year 181or 182." Rev. Lily, a Jewish symbol. Mint? Date 130-132 BC.[59]

2) Aristobulus I: Obv. "Yehudah the High Priest and the Council of the Jews." Rev. Double cornucopia adorned with ribbons, pomegranate between horns.

3) Alexander Jannaeus: Obv. "Yehonatan the High Priest and the Council of the Jews". Rev. Double cornucopia adorned with ribbons and a pomegranate between horns. It is thought, by some, that the lead "coin" may have been a token. Many, but not this one, had no striking on the back.

4) John Hyrcanus II: Obv. "Yonatan the High Priest and the Council of the Jews." Rev. Double cornucopia adorned with ribbons and a pomegranate between horns.

5) Judah Aristobulus II: Obv. "Yehudah the High Priest and Council of the Jews." Rev. Double cornucopia adorned with ribbons and pomegranate arising between the horns. There is some controversy that Aristobulus II did not mint coins.[60]

6) Mattathias Antigonus: Obv. Double cornucopia with Hebrew inscription "Matatayah the High Priest and Council of the Jews." Rev. Ivy wreath tied with ribbons and Greek inscription for King Antigonus. 8 Prutah coin.

---

[57] "The name Yehohanan consists of two distinct elements, the first one being יה (Yah) = יהו (Yahu) = יו (Yu), which in turn are abbreviated forms of the Tetragrammaton יהוה, YHWH, or Yahweh. The second element of our name comes from the verb חנן (hanan), meaning to be gracious." From: http://www.abarim-publications.com /Meaning/ Jehohanan .html#. VDvqffldWPI

[58] **SYMBOLS ON HASMONEAN DYNASTY COINS The Lily:** regarded as the choicest among the flowers. It graced the capitals of the two main pillars which stood at the entrance to the sanctuary. **The Pomegranate:** one of the seven celebrated products of Palestine and among the fruits brought to the temple as offerings of the first-fruits. Two hundred pomegranates decorated each of the two columns in the temple and were an integral part of the sacred vestment of the High Priest, as bells and pomegranates were suspended from his mantle. **The Cornucopia:** a hollow animal horn used as a container. One of the most popular religious symbols of the ancient world, the cornucopia is also known as the "horn of plenty." **The Anchor:** adopted from the Selukids, who used it to symbolize their naval strength. Anchors are depicted upside down, as they would be seen hung on the side of a boat ready for use. **The Star:** symbolizes heaven. **The Diadem:** symbolized royalty. http://www.forumancientcoins.com/catalog/roman-and-greek-coins. online 5-17-15. Information from the Handbook of Biblical Numismatics, American Numismatics Society online 12-2015.

[59] "The controversy revolved around the question of which Jewish ruler was the first to issue coins in his own name. For the first time in the modern era the world's top experts agree: It was John Hyrcanus I (135 – 104 BC), the son of Simon and nephew of the legendary Judah (Judas) Maccabeus, hero of the Chanukah story." http://coinproject.com/jan/volume1/issue1/volume1-1-3.html. That coin is not the one shown.

[60] Hendin, D. New Data Sheds Light on Hasmonean Coin Theories. J. Ancient Numismatics Vol.1:1 (Ap./May 2008).

The Hasmoneans
(Family of Maccabeans with Date of Rule)

John Hyrcanus I (135-104 BC)

Aristobulus I (104-103 BC)

Lead   Bronze

Alexander Jannaeus (Yehonatan 103-76 BC)

Salome Alexandra (76-67 BC she had no coins)

John Hyrcanus II (Yehohanan 67 and 63-40 BC)

Judah Aristobulus II (Yehudah 67-63 BC)

Mattahias Antigonus (40-37 BC)

coins not to relative scale

Hasmonean Prutah and Lepta

Many of the Hasmonean Prutah and lepta (1/2 Prutah) were poorly made. As mentioned before: the process of making coins included casting coin in strips which were then cut into round (more or less) planchettes. These were then stamped with an intaglio on the obverse and reverse. Below are examples where this process was poorly done:

(A) Sometimes the pouring into the molds may not have been complete.[61]

(B) Coins were at times double stamped on one or both sides, un-evenly stamped, or almost missing the planchette completely (not shown). Sometimes only one side was stamped (see legend on lead coins).

(C) Lepta were frequently poorly cast, stamped and then cut (see process at beginning of book).

Alexander Janneaus Image
by Guillaume Rouille (1518-1589)

---

[61] Some of the coins may simply have been eroded, but the smooth edge around the entire convoluted surfaces argues against this.

Hasmonean Prutah and Lepta
(Poorly Made)

A

B

C

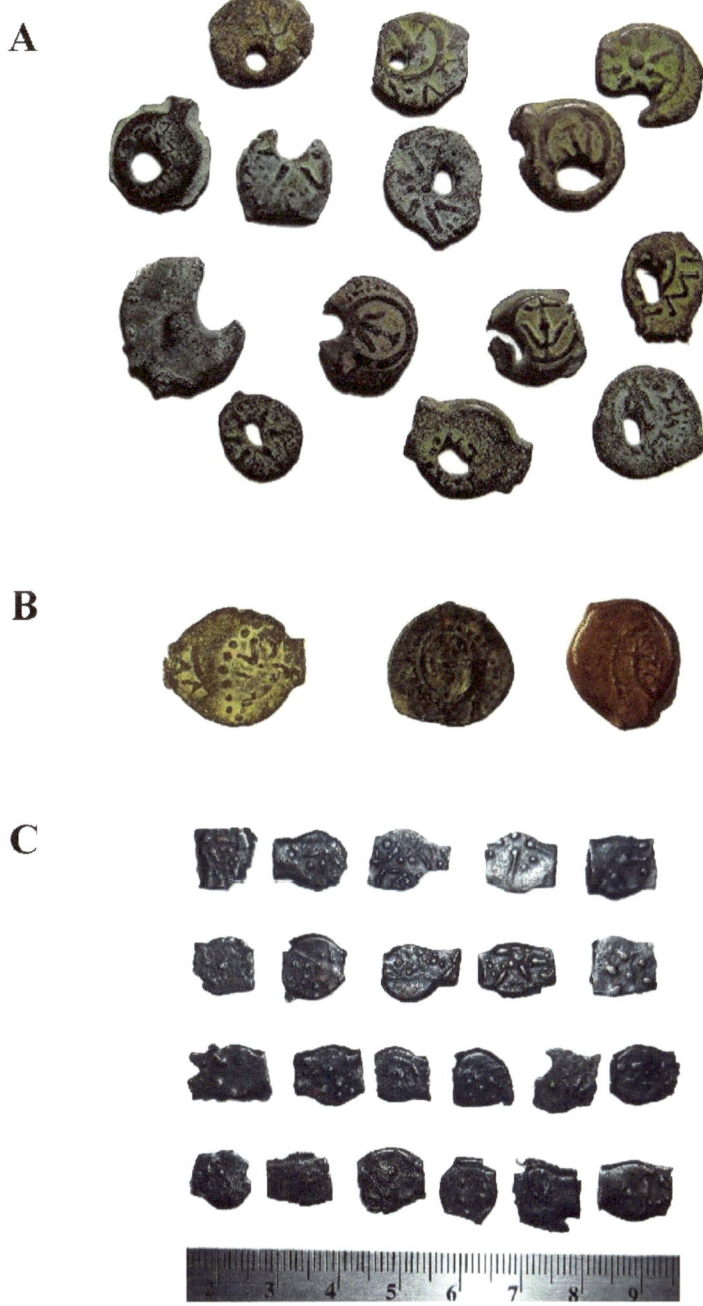

CHAPTER 7   THE ROMAN PERIOD IN JUDEA AND SURROUNDING AREA

Antipater, an Idumean, and His Relationship with the Romans
(Born?-Died 43 BC)

"But there was a certain friend of Hyrcanus II an Idumaean, called Antipater, who was very rich and in his nature an active and seditious man; who was at enmity with Aristobulus II, and had differences with him on account of his good will with Hyrcanus II…Antipater was suspicious of the power of Aristobulus…so he stirred up the most powerful of the Jews…"[62]

When Aristobulus II was attempting to overtake Hyrcanus II as king and High Priest in Judea, Antipater advised Hyrcanus II to flee to the Nabatean King Aretas at Petra. Antipater had previously married a Nabatean noblewoman and thus knew the king. He later returned with Hyrcanus II to Judea when Hyrcanus II was placed in power there by the Romans.[63]

Antipater was involved in intrigue throughout his life and it was all centered on gaining power. He was adept at assessing situations and adapting and associating himself with whomever he felt would be the new authority in any given situation. Initially, he aligned with the Roman general Pompey, but then later with Julius Caesar.

---

[62] Josephus Antiquities of the Jews Book XIV Chapter 1.
[63] "Antipater, who seems to have succeeded his father as governor of Idumæa, had reason to fear that King Aristobulus II. would not retain him in his position. He therefore tried his utmost to dethrone Aristobulus, and to restore the weak Hyrcanus II., who would be an easy tool in his hands, to the throne which was rightfully his. With this view Antipater tried to persuade Hyrcanus, who was not only of a peaceful and kindly disposition but altogether free from suspicion, that his brother was plotting his death in order to secure himself upon the throne. Hyrcanus at first refused credence to Antipater, but finally allowed himself to be gained over. Antipater, who felt no attachment for Judaism or the Jewish state, and who stood ready to sacrifice their interests in order to serve his own ends, had made previous arrangements with Aretas, an Arabian chief, to give his help to Hyrcanus in return for a large sum of money and possession of twelve cities, which had been conquered from the Arabians by the Hasmoneans after long and hard fighting. Antipater then took Hyrcanus with him to Aretas, who forthwith proceeded with a large army against Aristobulus, and defeated him. Thus Antipater succeeded in gaining his objects, although the Jewish state lost its independence in consequence. The dispute was referred to Rome, and decision was given against Aristobulus…The remnant of independence which Pompey had allowed to Judea, whose nominal king was now Hyrcanus II., proved of great advantage to Antipater, as he now held Hyrcanus completely under his control."
http://jewishencyclopedia.com/articles/1598-antipater

Grayzel has commented, "Antipater and Rome, from this time on worked together."[64] Pompey placed Antipater as administer of Judea. And Antipater then placed two of his sons Phasael and Herod 1st as governors of Jerusalem and Galilee.[65]

Antipater incurred the hate of the Jewish population for his regard for Greek and Roman things and an open disregard of Jewish things. In the end he died by poisoning.[66] Yet, he had set the stage and had trained his offspring in the habits/customs/beliefs that they would later be involved in, especially his son Herod 1st who would become Herod the Great.

Temple of Zeus   Jerash, Jordan

---

[64] Grayzel on pg. 88 would further comment; "Both (Antipater and Pompey) were greedy for power, and both felt the hostility of the people (the Jews) directed against them. As a result, no matter what political mistakes the Idumaeans made, Rome always forgave them. On the other hand, no matter what demands Rome made Antipater and his sons always fulfilled them. Hyrcanus II…was nothing more than a puppet. Actually Antipater ruled and two of his sons, Phasael and Herod 1st…"
[65] Wikipedia on "Antipater the Idumean". Online 2-17-15.
[66] "Cassius promised him also, that after the war was over, he would make him king of Judea. But it so happened that the power and hopes of his son became the cause of his perdition; for as Malichus was afraid of this, he corrupted one of the king's cup-bearers with money to give a poisoned potion to Antipater; so he became a sacrifice to Malichus's wickedness, and died at a feast." Josephus Wars Book 1.11.4.

The Nabataeans

The Nabataeans[67] were a powerful Middle East group, probably an amalgam of several different Arabic groups. They were known for trading, especially in expensive spices like frankincense and myrrh. They developed sophisticated water storage systems in a very arid part of the world, and along a major trade route. They became very wealthy.

The origin of their ancestors is still debated, but there was a group mentioned in the annals of King Assurbanipal (668-627 BC) with the name of Na-baiab-Nabaiati that were located in Babylonia. Josephus associates them with the offspring of Ishmael. From the findings of their writings they covered a large area from the Sinai, Petra, Oultre Jourdain, to some parts of Syria.

They had numerous interactions with the Hasmoneans, sometimes in friendship (Judas Maccabeus), sometimes in battle (Alexander Jannaeus was defeated in 82 BC) and as joined forces (against the Romans with Hyrcanus II in 67 BC).

A key leader, and one who had interaction in several events in the Bible during the times of Christ was Aretas IV (9 BC-40 AD). The previous Nabatean ruler Obodas III was assassinated and Aretas assumed the crown, though he was not next in line. He called himself "Aretas, King of the Nabataeans, Friend of his People".[68] He is important in Mark 6:17-20 as Herod Antipas who married his daughter planned to divorce her for Herodias. Aretas entered Herod Antipas and Phillip's land and defeated them and took some of it in reprisal. As well, Paul is lowered in a basket when in Damascus, as officials were seeking to take him. Aretas apparently had control of this area. (2 Corinthians 11:32-3; Acts 9:21-26).

He is important in an event where Aristobulus II was attempting to imprison or kill his relative, Hyracanus II, the legal heir to the throne. Antipater the Idumaean took him to Aretas for safety. Later, Antipater would return to Jerusalem with Hyrcanus II when the Romans put Hyrcanus in authority. Antipater through intrigue would grow in influence in Jerusalem and follow after Hyrcanus. However, the Nabataeans would diminish in power and wealth and came under Roman authority.

---

[67] The Nabataeans Through Their Inscriptions by Francisco Del Rio Sanchez at www.academic.edu/6798331 online 7-1-2015.
[68] Wikipedia: Aretas IV Philopatris online 7-1-2015.

The Nabatean Kingdom and Its Relationship to Judea

**Aretas and Shaqilat
Nabatean King and Queen
9BC-40AD**

**The Treasury at
Entrance to Petra**

The Herods

The Herods were leaders in the region of Canaan (Judea) during the times of Jesus Christ.

Herod 1st The Great (74/3 BC - 4/3 BC)

Herod 1st began this dynasty. He was a Jew by his father (Antipater) who had been forcibly converted to Judaism as a child[69] by the Hasmonean leaders. He seemed to oppose Jewish beliefs his entire life. He was a ruthless man as were many of his offspring. His power came through appointment by Caesar Augustus in 40 BC as an ethnarch. Herod then became a "king of Judea" after overthrowing the Hasmonean king Mattathias Antigonus with the help of the Roman general Sossius in 37 BC. He had Antigonus executed along with Hyrcanus II (another Hasmonean leader), and later he would kill Aristobulus II. Thus he removed any claim to the throne by a Hasmonean.[70] He married 3 times. He was born 74/3 BC in Idumæa (south of Judea) and was a Nabatean by genealogy. He hellenized the area by introducing Greek customs. See Scripture relating to him:

> Matthew 2:1 "Now after Jesus was born in Bethlehem of Judea in the days of Herod the king, magi from the east arrived in Jerusalem, saying, ² "Where is He who has been born King of the Jews? For we saw His star in the east and have come to worship Him." ³ When **Herod the king** heard *this*, he was troubled, and all Jerusalem with him. … ¹³ Now when they had gone, behold, an angel of the Lord appeared to Joseph in a dream and said, "Get up! Take the Child and His mother and flee to Egypt, and remain there until I tell you; for **Herod** is going to search for the Child to destroy Him."… ¹⁶ Then when **Herod** saw that he had been tricked by the magi, he became very enraged, and sent and slew all the male children who were in Bethlehem and all its vicinity, from two years old and under, according to the time which he had determined from the magi."

Herod also offended the Jewish people when he put a statue of an eagle, the symbol of Rome, on the Temple area. He celebrated this by putting an eagle on one of his coins. (See Herodian Coins)

Herod Archelaus (23 BC-18 AD)

Archelaus, a son of Herod 1st, was made ethnarch over Samaria, Judea, and Idumæa by Augustus after the death of Herod the Great. However, he was a harsh ruler and after the slaughter of 3,000 people during a protest in Jerusalem, Jewish leaders went to Rome to protest his actions. His rulership was taken away and given to Antipas. He was banished to Vienna in Gaul after only nine years of rule 4 BC-6 AD.

> Matthew 2¹⁹ "But when Herod died, behold, an angel of the Lord appeared in a dream to Joseph in Egypt, and said, ²⁰ "Get up, take the Child and His mother, and go into the land of Israel; for those who sought the Child's life are dead." ²¹ So Joseph got up, took the Child and His mother, and came into the land of Israel. ²² But when he heard that **Archelaus** was reigning over Judea in place of his father Herod, he was afraid to go there. Then after being warned *by God* in a dream, he left for the regions of Galilee, ²³ and came and lived in a city called Nazareth. *This was* to fulfill what was spoken through the prophets: "He shall be called a Nazarene."

---

[69] D. Hendin Guide to Biblical Coins, 1987, Amphora Books, pg. 59.
[70] **Hasmonean dynasty** (hæzməˈniːən/; Hebrew: חשמונאים, Roman. *Ḥashmonaʼim*) was the ruling dynasty of Judea…" fr. Wikipedia. Semi-autonomous 140-110 BC. In 110 BC revolt against the Seleucids was successful, autonomous to 110-37 BC. Conquered by Rome and the Herods were put into power 37 BC.

Herod Antipas (before 20 BC-40 AD)

Antipas was another son of Herod 1st and he was educated in Rome with his brothers. He is also the one who was ruling in Galilee, Perea, and a portion of the Transjordan (4 BC-39 AD) when John the Baptist was preaching in the Wilderness. In front of him Herodias danced and asked for the head of John the Baptist. Antipas was called "that fox" by Jesus Luke 13:31-32. He was designated a tetrarch by Augustus, and lived in Sepphoris and then Tiberias, and was given Galilee and Perea.[71] In 40 AD he was banished to Lugdunum in Gaul by Caesar Caligula for treason based on accusations by Agrippa 1. See Scripture referring to his role in the death of Jesus Christ.

> Luke 13:31-32 "Just at that time some Pharisees approached, saying to Him, 'Go away, leave here, for Herod wants to kill You.' And He said to them, "Go and tell that fox, 'Behold, I cast out demons and perform cures today and tomorrow, and the third *day* I reach My goal'."

It was also Antipas that Jesus Christ was brought before for trial (as well as with Pilate). See Luke 23:1-12.

> Luke 23:1 "Then the whole body of them got up and brought Him before Pilate. ² And they began to accuse Him, saying, "We found this man misleading our nation and forbidding to pay taxes to Caesar, and saying that He Himself is Christ, a King." ³ So Pilate asked Him, saying, "Are You the King of the Jews?" And He answered him and said, "*It is as* you say." ⁴ Then Pilate said to the chief priests and the crowds, "I find no guilt in this man." … ⁶ When Pilate heard it, he asked whether the man was a **Galilean**. ⁷ And when he learned that He belonged to **Herod's jurisdiction**, he sent Him to **Herod**, who himself also was in Jerusalem at that time. … ⁹ And he questioned Him at some length; but He answered him nothing. ¹⁰ And the chief priests and the scribes were standing there, accusing Him vehemently. ¹¹ And Herod with his soldiers, after treating Him with contempt and mocking Him, dressed Him in a gorgeous robe and sent Him back to Pilate. ¹² Now Herod and Pilate became friends with one another that very day; for before they had been enemies with each other."

Herod Philip 2 (27 BC-34 AD)

Philip, a third son of Herod 1st, received as an inheritance after Herod 1st death in 4 BC, the areas of Gaulanitis, Trachonitis, Aurantis, Batanaea, and Paneas. Most of the populous were non-Jewish. His coins had his image stamped on them, which would have offended Jewish peoples but not the gentiles. He built up the city of Paneas which was then called Caesarea after Augustus and later it became Caesarea Philipi. There he built a temple dedicated to Augustus called the Augusteum and it is featured on his coins (see the coin figure).[72] His mother was Cleopatra of Jerusalem (not Egyptian). He is mentioned in the scriptures:

> Luke 3:1 "Now in the fifteenth year of the reign of **Tiberius Caesar**, when **Pontius Pilate** was governor of Judea, and **Herod was tetrarch of Galilee**, and **his brother Philip was tetrarch of the region of Iturae**a and Trachonitis, and Lysanias was tetrarch of Abilene …"

> Matt. 14:3 "For when Herod had John arrested, he bound him and put him in prison because of Herodias, the wife of his brother Philip. ⁴ For John had been saying to him, 'It is not lawful for you to have her'."

---

[71] Ibid Hendin, pg. 67.
[72] Meshorer: A Treasure of Jewish Coins, 2001, pg. 85.

Herod Philip's wife, Herodias, would leave him (as mentioned earlier) and would go to Herod Antipas. She was instrumental in having John the Baptist's head cut off as he had spoken against her union with Antipas.[73,74]

Jesus before Herod Antipas, Albrecht Durer, 1509.

---

[73] Matt. 14: ³"For when Herod had John arrested, he bound him and put him in prison because of Herodias, the wife of his brother Philip. ⁴For John had been saying to him, 'It is not lawful for you to have her'."

[74] This occurred at Machaerus. See map and photo on adjoining page.

Machaerus-Jordan

(John the Baptist beheaded by Herod Antipas at this site.)

The Division of Herod the Great's Kingdom after His Death

"Antipas was not Herod's first choice of heir. That honor fell to **Aristobulus and Alexander**, Herod's sons by the Hasmonean princess Mariamne. It was only after they were executed (c.7 BC), and Herod's oldest son **Antipater** was convicted of trying to poison his father (5 BC), that the now elderly Herod fell back on his youngest son **Antipas**, revising his will to make him heir. During his fatal illness in 4 BC, Herod had yet another change of heart about the succession. According to the final version of his will, Antipas' elder brother **Archelaus** was now to become king of Judea, Idumea and Samaria, while **Antipas** would rule Galilee and Perea with the lesser title of tetrarch. **Philip** was to receive Gaulanitis (the Golan Heights), Batanaea (southern Syria), Trachonitis and Auranitis (Hauran)." [75,76]

See map next page for approximate divisions of Herod's Kingdom.

Herod Antipas – Maroon

Herod Philip 2 - Orange

Herod Archelaus - Green

---

[75] Wikipedia Herod Antipas http://en.wikipedia.org/wiki/Herod_Antipas#cite_note-7

[76] [188] "and now Herod altered his testament upon the alteration of his mind; for he appointed Antipas, to whom he had before left the kingdom, to be tetrarch of Galilee and Perea, and granted the kingdom to Archclaus. He also gave Gaulonitis, and Trachonitis, and Paneas to Philip, who was his son, but own brother to Archclaus by the name of a tetrarchy; and bequeathed Jarnnia, and Ashdod, and Phasaelis to Salome his sister, with five hundred thousand [drachmae] of silver that was coined…When it is here said that Philip the tetrarch, and Archelaus the king, or ethnarch, were own brother, or genuine brothers, if those words mean own brothers, or born of the same father and mother, there must be here some mistake; because they had indeed the same father, Herod, but different mothers; the former Cleopatra, and Archclaus Malthace." Josephus, *Antiquities* 17.188–189.

Herod's Territories After Herod 1st Death

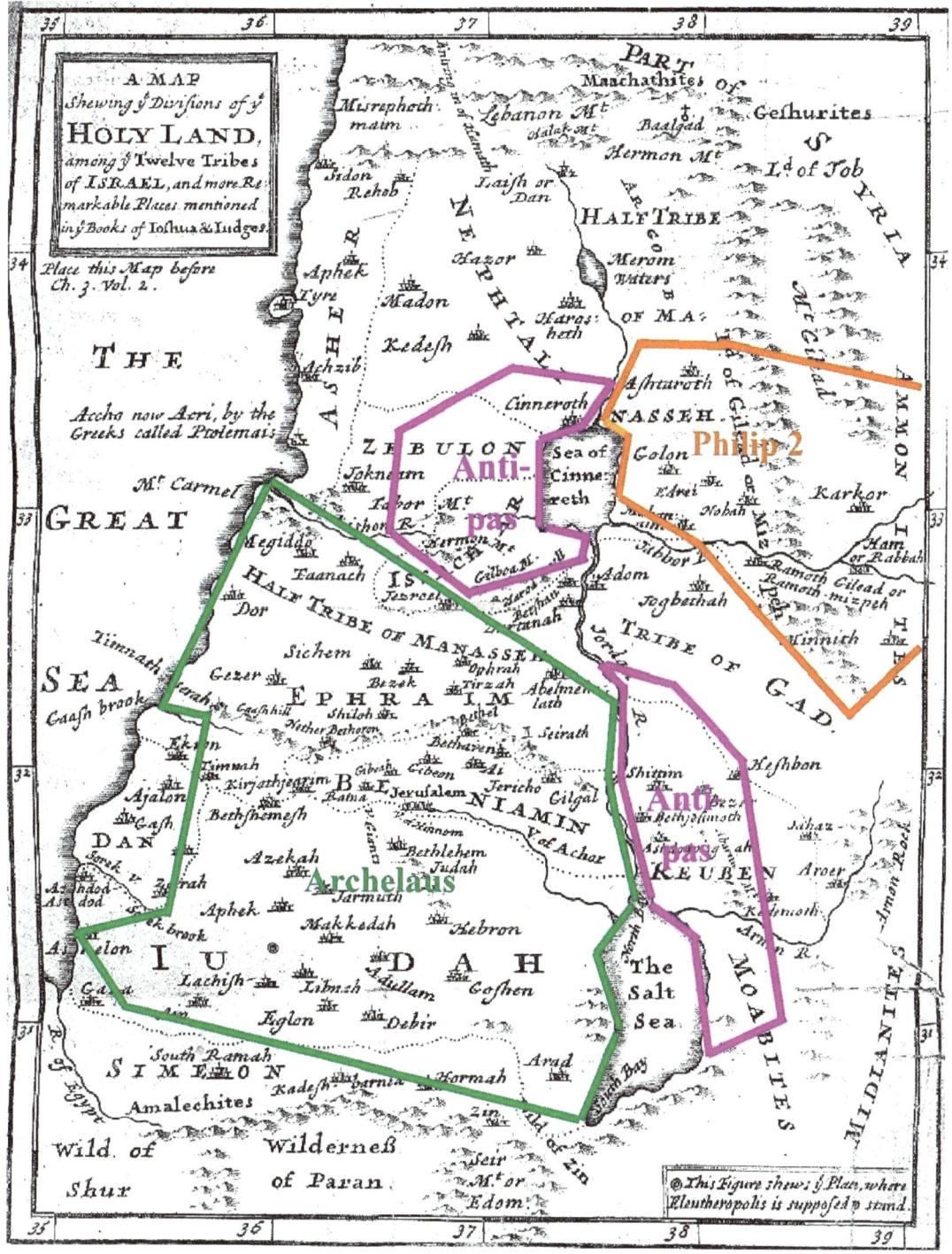

Herod Agrippa 1 (11-44 AD)

Agrippa 1 was the grandson of Herod the Great and Mariamne (Hasmonean), and son of Aristobulus (whom Herod 1 executed). He was educated in Rome along with other relatives. He was put in prison by Tiberius for "treasonous" thoughts, but released by Caligulia in 37 A.D. and placed in charge of areas that had previously been governed by his uncle Herod Philip. Agrippa was much involved in intrigue all of his life and was even involved in the banishment of his uncle Herod Antipas. He was a supporter of the Jewish people, and built up fortifications around Jerusalem, but opposed Christianity. In Acts 12:1-8 it refers to him:

> ^{1} Now about that time Herod the king laid hands on some who belonged to the church in order to mistreat them. ^{2} And he had James the brother of John put to death with a sword. ^{3} When he saw that it pleased the Jews, he proceeded to arrest Peter also. Now it was during the days of Unleavened Bread. ^{4} When he had seized him, he put him in prison, delivering him to four squads of soldiers to guard him, intending after the Passover to bring him out before the people. ^{5} So Peter was kept in the prison, but prayer for him was being made fervently by the church to God. ^{6} On the very night when Herod was about to bring him forward, Peter was sleeping between two soldiers, bound with two chains, and guards in front of the door were watching over the prison. ^{7} And behold, an angel of the Lord suddenly appeared and a light shone in the cell; and he struck Peter's side and woke him up, saying, "Get up quickly." And his chains fell off his hands. ^{8} And the angel said to him, "Gird yourself and put on your sandals." And he did so. And he said to him, 'Wrap your cloak around you and follow me."

So Peter was delivered from Herod Agrippa. Agrippa's death was dramatic. While giving a speech in Caesarea at an event honoring the Caesar Josephus records: "At this festival a great number were gathered of the principal persons of dignity of his province….he put on a garment wholly made of silver…illuminated by the fresh reflection of the sun's rays, shone out in a wonderful manner…flatters cried out…that he was a god; and they added, 'Be thou merciful to us; for although we have hitherto reverenced thee only as a man, yet shall we henceforth own thee as superior to mortal nature.' Upon this the king neither rebuked them nor rejected their impious flattery…A severe pain arose in his belly, striking with the most violet intensity…And when he had been quite worn out by the pain in his belly for five days, he departed this life…"[77]

Acts 12:21 says:

> ^{21} On an appointed day Herod, having put on his royal apparel, took his seat on the rostrum and *began* delivering an address to them. ^{22} The people kept crying out, "The voice of a god and not of a man!" ^{23} And immediately an angel of the Lord struck him because he did not give God the glory, and he was eaten by worms and died.

---

[77] Josephus Antiquities 19.8.2 343-361.

Herod Agrippa 2 (27-95 AD)

Agrippa 2, the son of Agrippa 1, was only 17 years old and living in Rome when his father died in 44 AD. He was not given rulership till Herod of Chalis died in 48 AD. He then was given his territory and expanded to have Herod Philip's old territory by Caesar Claudius. Caesar Nero next gave him other northern territories including Tiberias in Galilee, and supervision of the Temple Mount in Jerusalem and the appointing of the High Priest. His handling of the High Priest brought him into disfavor with the Jewish people. When there were murmurings of revolt against the Roman government he encouraged them not to. He also had an incestuous relationship with his sister Bernice who also had a long relationship with the Roman General Titus. He and Bernice were expelled from Jerusalem in 66 AD, and per one report he actually assisted Vespasian where Agrippa was injured at the Battle of Gamla. He and Bernice then moved to Rome.[78]

He is mentioned in the Bible as one of the leaders Paul made a presentation to in Acts 25:13-27 and 26:1-32:

> **25** [13] Now when several days had elapsed, King Agrippa and Bernice arrived at Caesarea and paid their respects to Festus. [14] While they were spending many days there, Festus laid Paul's case before the king, saying, "There is a man who was left as a prisoner by Felix; [15] and when I was at Jerusalem, the chief priests and the elders of the Jews brought charges against him, asking for a sentence of condemnation against him. ... [18] When the accusers stood up, they *began* bringing charges against him not of such crimes as I was expecting, [19] but they *simply* had some points of disagreement with him about their own religion and about a dead man, Jesus, whom Paul asserted to be alive. ... [22] Then Agrippa *said* to Festus, "I also would like to hear the man myself." "Tomorrow," he said, "you shall hear him." [23] So, on the next day when Agrippa came together with Bernice amid great pomp, and entered the auditorium accompanied by the commanders and the prominent men of the city, at the command of Festus, Paul was brought in. [24] Festus said, "King Agrippa, and all you gentlemen here present with us, you see this man about whom all the people of the Jews appealed to me, both at Jerusalem and here, loudly declaring that he ought not to live any longer. [25] But I found that he had committed nothing worthy of death; and since he himself appealed to the Emperor, I decided to send him. [26] Yet I have nothing definite about him to write to my lord. Therefore I have brought him before you *all* and especially before you, King Agrippa, so that after the investigation has taken place, I may have something to write. [27] For it seems absurd to me in sending a prisoner, not to indicate also the charges against him." **26** Agrippa said to Paul, "You are permitted to speak for yourself." Then Paul stretched out his hand and *proceeded* to make his defense: [2] "In regard to all the things of which I am accused by the Jews, I consider myself fortunate, King Agrippa, that I am about to make my defense before you today; [3] especially because you are an expert in all customs and questions among *the* Jews; therefore I beg you to listen to me patiently. ... [23] that the Christ was to suffer, *and* that by reason of *His* resurrection from the dead He would be the first to proclaim light both to the *Jewish* people and to the Gentiles."
> [24] While *Paul* was saying this in his defense, Festus *said in a loud voice, "Paul, you are out of your mind! *Your* great learning is driving you mad." [25] But Paul said, "I am not out of my mind, most excellent Festus, but I utter words of sober truth. [26] For the king knows about these matters, and I speak to him also with confidence, since I am persuaded that none of these things escape his notice; for this has not been done in a corner. [27] King Agrippa, do you believe the Prophets? I know that you do." [28] Agrippa *replied* to Paul, "In a short time you will persuade me to become a Christian." ... [32] And Agrippa said to Festus, "This man might have been set free if he had not appealed to Caesar."

---

[78] Wikipedia Herod Agrippa 2 online 1-17-2015.

Herod Agrippa II

From: Guillaume Rouille 1553 AD

THE LINEAGE OF THE HERODS

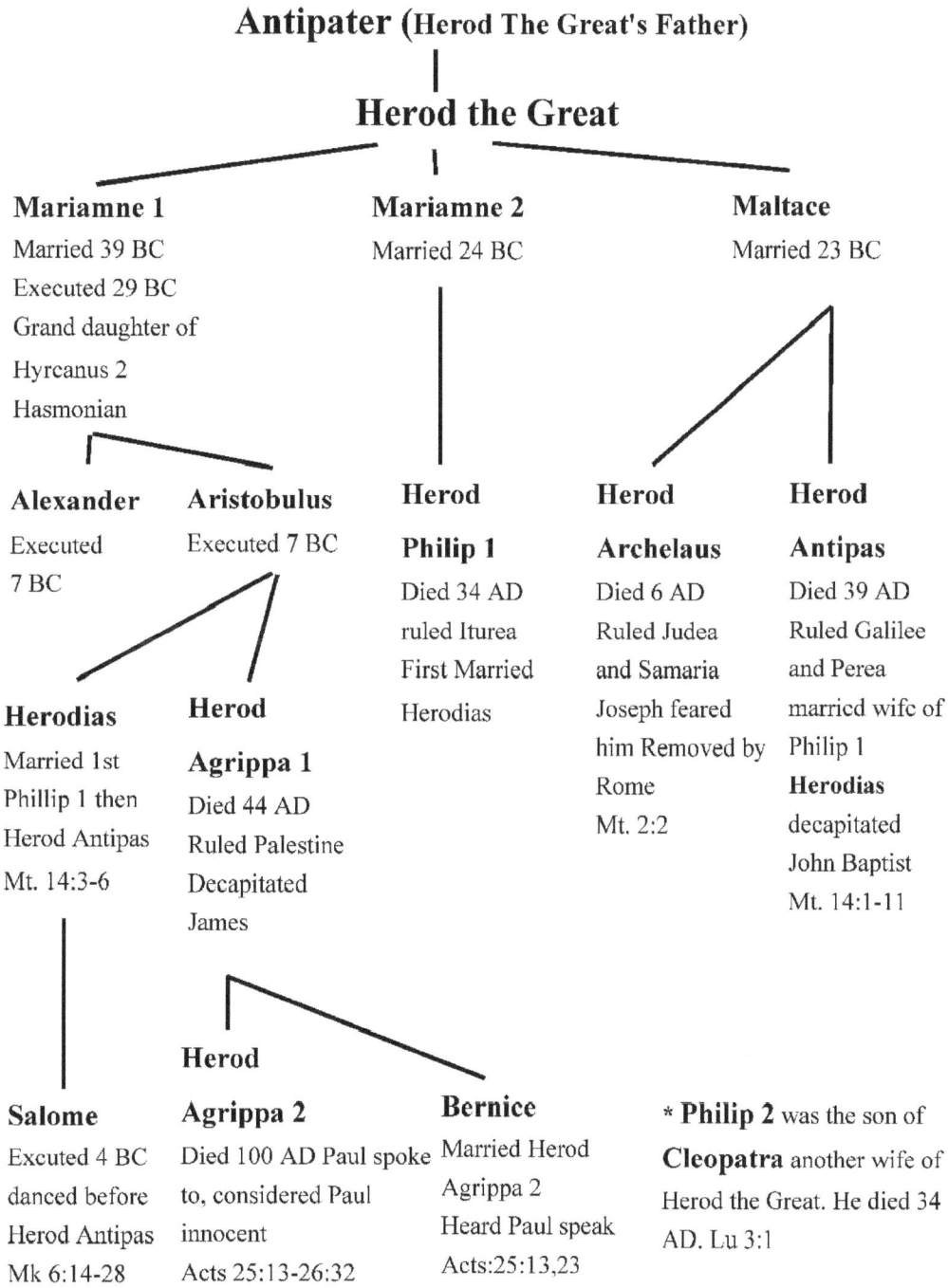

Herodian Coins

Herod 1

Coin: Herod 1st 8 prutot obv.(shown) Tripod with ceremonial bowl dated LΓ year 3 or 40 B.C. Has Greek inscription ΒΑΣΙΛΕΩΣ ΗΡΩΔΥ "of King Herod".[79] The rev. has Thymiateron (incense burner). Note: no graven image yet.

Coin: Herod 1st lepton obv. Anchor with Greek inscription ΒΑCΙΛΗΡWΔ (King Herod). Rev. Eagle standing to the Right. "This is apparently the first coin issued by a Jewish ruler for use by Jews with a graven image upon it."[80]

Herod Archelaus

Coin: Herod Archelaus Prutah obv. Brow of ship Greek inscription ΗΡW. Rev. (shown) Greek inscription ΕθΝ (ethnarch) with wreath and dots.

Herod Antipas

Coin: Herod Antipas ½ denomination obv. (shown) Palm branch and Greek Lettering LKΔ (Year 24) and ΗΡWΔΟΤΕΤΡ (of Herod the Tetrarch)[81] rev. ΤΙΒC ΡΙΑC (Tiberius Ruler) with wreath.

Herod Philip

Coin: Herod Phllip 2 obv. Head of Tiberius to right and with stamp. Rev. Tetrastyle temple with LΛZ year 37 or 33/34 AD.

Herod Agrippa 1

Coin: obv. Umbrella with inscription ΒΑCΙΛΕWC ΑΓΡΙΠΑ. rev. Three ears of barley between two leaves with LS (year 6 or 42/43 AD)[82]

Herod Agrippa 2

Coin: obv. Laurette head Nero with inscription ΝΕΡΩΝ ΚΑΙCΑΡΣΕΒΑΣΤ (Nero Caesar Augustus) rev. Inscription ΕΠΙ ΒΑCΙΛΕ ΑΓΡΙΠΠΙ ΝΕΡΩΝΙ Ε (E=year 5 or 61 AD)[83]

---

[79] Y. Meshorer A Treasury of Jewish Coins, 2001, Amphora Books, pg. 62.
[80] Ibid Hendin pg. 56.
[81] Ibid Hendin, pg. 68.
[82] Ibid Hendin, pg. 72.
[83] Ibid Hendin, pg. 76.

The Herods

Herod 1 (The Great)

(Coins are not to relative scale.)

Herod Agrippa 1
of Idumean and Hasmonean Lineage

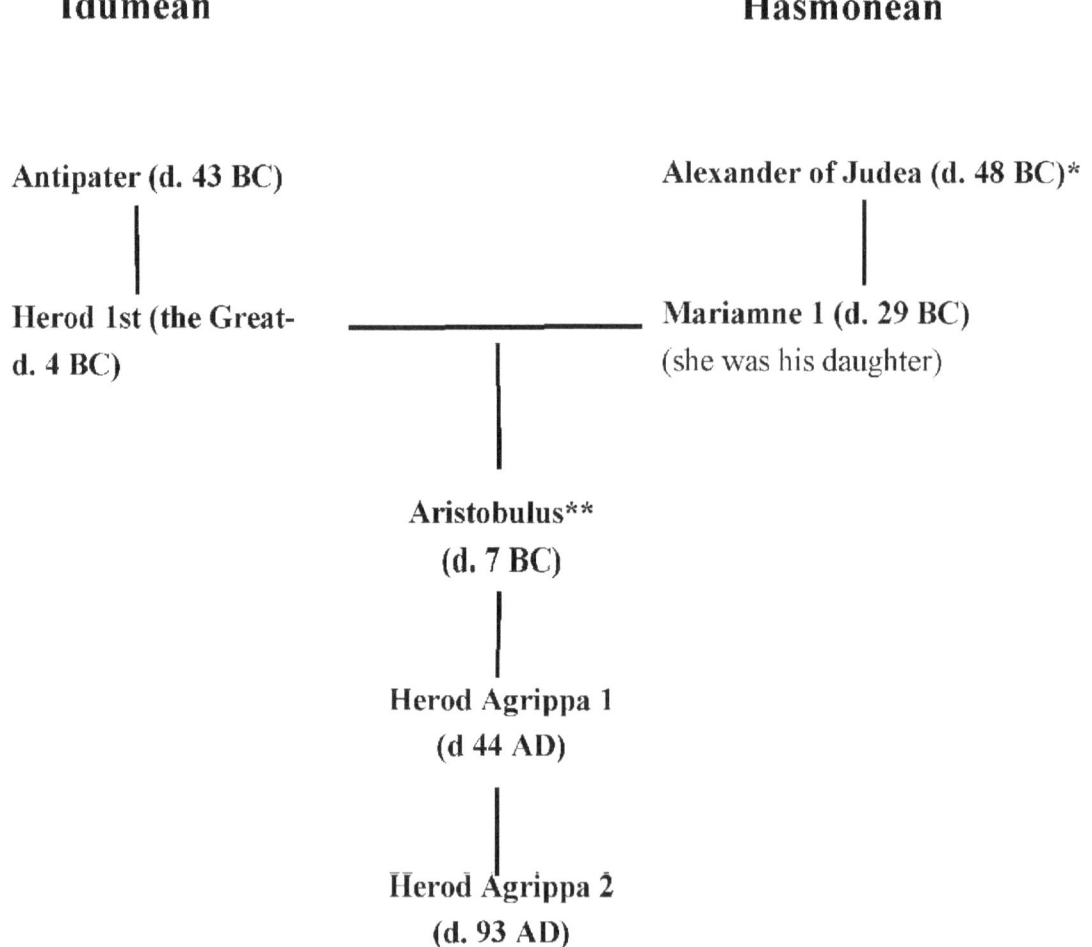

* Alexander of Judea was a son of Aristobulus 2 of Hasmonean lineage. On his mother's side was Alexandra daughter of Hyracanus 2 also Hasmonean. Hyrcanus 2 was executed by Herod the Great in 30 BC.

** Aristobulus, not to be confused with the pure lineage Hasmonean leader was executed by Herod the Great in 7 BC.

Chart derived from: https://en.wikipedia.org/wiki/Herod_Agrippa_II

Herod Agrippa 1 Sacrificing Pig with Claudius

Obv. TIBEPIOO KAICAP OBEBAOTOO AEOM (Tiberius Ceasar Augustus Germannicus) in Greek.

Claudius and **Agrippa 1** stand on each side of sacrifice with patera in hands in tetrastyle temple. **Priest** in center with raised object-knife?

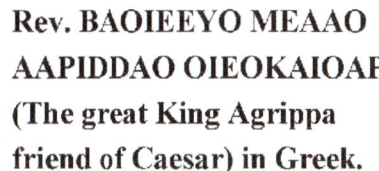

Rev. BAOIEEYO MEAAO AAPIDDAO OIEOKAIOAP (The great King Agrippa friend of Caesar) in Greek.

Victamarius kneeling and holding pig.

Documentation: Suetonius (Roman historian) The Twelve Caesars
"Whenever he concluded a treaty with foreign rulers, he sacrificed a sow in the Forum, using the ancient formula of the Fetial priests." From:Guttenberg.org online, Claudius section 25.

Documentation: Josephus Antiquities of the Jews
"Now when Claudius had taken out of the way all those soldiers whom he suspected, which he did immediately, he published an edict, and therein confirmed that kingdom to Agrippa which Caius had given him, and therein commended the king highly. He also made all addition to it of all that country over which Herod, who was his grandfather, had reigned, that is, Judea and Samaria; and this he restored to him as due to his family. But for Abila 16 of Lysanias, and all that lay at Mount Libanus, he bestowed them upon him, as out of his own territories. He also made a league with this Agrippa, confirmed by oaths, in the middle of the forum, in the city of Rome." From Guttenberg.org, Book xix 5:1. Coin image permit from www.forumancientcoins.com 2-9-15.

Roman Leaders in the Time of Christ Demonstrated by Coins of the Period

The times of Jesus Christ were turbulent. The scriptures clearly teach that the Messiah would be brought forth at the key moment in history.[84] Then His own people as a nation did not accept Him but the majority of early Christian believers were Jewish. As well, He and His teachings were rejected by the Roman leaders in the region. Tacitus called the Jewish faith a national superstition[85] (which would include Christians). He had trouble with a moral people who believed in a God they could not see. Josephus, a Jewish historian, wrote of Jesus Christ as a good teacher. Yet His teaching would have an ever expanding impact on the Roman Empire such that by the time of Constantine whole communities were Christian, and Constantine for complex reasons promoted Christianity as a state religion in the early 300's AD.

Jesus Christ was born when Caesar Augustus, Octavian, was ruler (about 3-4 BC).[86,87] Octavian had become the unquestioned sole leader of the Roman Empire acquiring it by military prowess and political intrigue. He established some social norms, unified the economy, and complied with the common polytheistic beliefs. He confirmed Herod the Great's position in Judea, and appointed Polonius the procurator in that area. It was Polonius and subsequent procurators who appointed the Jewish Temple's High Priest. Tribute was collected to support Roman military garrisons stationed throughout Israel. Occasional uprisings against Roman rule were quickly crushed. Upon Octavian's death the Romans elevated him to the level of being divine. This is reflected on coins listing his name as "Divi" Augustus. Tiberius, a relative, was then elected Caesar. It is said by Eusebius, a early church historian, that Christ's teaching were available to him. Eusebius said that this Caesar nominated Jesus as a god to the Roman Senate but that it was rejected. Sejanus, who was Tiberius' principal assistant, and was later tried for treason, did not persecute Christians but did target and persecute the Jewish people. Subsequent leaders such as Nero and Domitian would commit egregious crimes against both Jews and Christians, such as throwing them to lions to eat and burning them alive etc.

Jesus never spoke for revolting against the Roman government. Rather, in a poignant moment he

---

[84] Romans 5:6-8: ⁶For while we were still helpless, at the right time Christ died for the ungodly. ⁷For one will hardly die for a righteous man; though perhaps for the good man someone would dare even to die. ⁸But God demonstrates His own love toward us, in that while we were yet sinners, Christ died for us.

[85] "Such indeed were the precautions of human wisdom. The next thing was to seek means of propitiating the gods, and recourse was had to the Sibylline books, by the direction of which prayers were offered to Vulcanus, Ceres, and Proserpina. Juno, too, was entreated by the matrons, first, in the Capitol, then on the nearest part of the coast, whence water was procured to sprinkle the fane and image of the goddess. And there were sacred banquets and nightly vigils celebrated by married women. But all human efforts, all the lavish gifts of the emperor, and the propitiations of the gods, did not banish the sinister belief that the conflagration was the result of an order.

Consequently, to get rid of the report, Nero fastened the guilt and inflicted the most exquisite tortures on a class hated for their abominations, called Christians by the populace. Christus, from whom the name had its origin, suffered the extreme penalty during the reign of Tiberius at the hands of one of our procurators, Pontius Pilatus, **and a most mischievous superstition**, thus checked for the moment, again broke out not only in Judaea, the first source of the evil, but even in Rome, where all things hideous and shameful from every part of the world find their centre and become popular."
From: http://www.earlychristianwritings.com/tacitus.html In the Annals 15:44.

[86] Luke 2:1,4-7 "Now in those days a decree went out from Caesar Augustus, that a census be taken of all the inhabited earth. ... ⁴Joseph also went up from Galilee, from the city of Nazareth, to Judea, to the city of David which is called Bethlehem, because he was of the house and family of David, ⁵in order to register along with Mary, who was engaged to him, and was with child. ⁶While they were there, the days were completed for her to give birth. ⁷And she gave birth to her firstborn son; and she wrapped Him in cloths, and laid Him in a manger… "

[87] "Yeshua was born on the 15th day of 7th month of the biblical calendar, the first day of the Feast of Tabernacles (a High Sabbath), which always occurs in autumn. On the Julian calendar, it was Thursday, September 26, 3 BC."
https://www.facebook.com/michael.j.rood/posts/10151931476349177

stated using a Roman denarius with Caesars' image on it, to render unto Caesar the things that are Caesars' and unto God the things that are His. Yet, He also did not violate the attitude of Hebrew princes who refused to bow to the golden image in Babylon, as He fulfilled all righteousness.

In our day both Jewish and Christian leaders lament the infiltration of secular mindsets and living into their synagogues and churches. Jesus Christ had to deal with the same sorts of attitudes. His attention was always on the issues of the heart. Thus He used a whip against the money changers who had changed the Temple area into a "den of thieves". They charged excess rates of exchange to convert foreign currency into the Tyre shekel which was the only accepted coin used for the Temple tax. They also charged a larger than needed fee for purchasing acceptable pigeons and other animals used in the offerings and sacrifices. With the woman caught in the act of adultery Jesus exposed the hearts of those who were about to stone her, and brought her to a place of repentance and forgiveness.[88]

When Jesus was taken to the cross He was condemned by the authorities of the Temple High Priest, the local Idumean leader Antipas, and the Roman procurator Pontius Pilate. After His death both Jews and Christians were increasingly persecuted locally and regionally. James a brother of Jesus was killed by Herod Agrippa I. Paul the Apostle was interrogated by Procurator Felix, then by Festus, and even Herod Agrippa II while he continued in prison. His appeal to Caesar, under Roman Law, referred him to Nero who subsequently had him beheaded. The Jewish War of 66-70 AD, the Bar Kochba Rebellion of 132-135 AD resulted in the expulsion of the Jews and Jewish Christians from Jerusalem. For Christians this accelerated the spread of Christ's teachings across all the Roman Empire; a direct fulfillment of His commandment to "go into all the earth and preach the gospel, and make disciples of men" (Mark 16). The Jews, however, would not return to control at least part of their land again until the "end of the age" as prophesied in the books of Isaiah, Ezekiel, Zephaniah, and others. This began to happen in the early 1900's AD with the Jewish nation re-established in 1948, approximately two thousand years later. Modern Israeli coinage reflects this theme.

---

[88] John 8:1-11: "¹But Jesus went to the Mount of Olives. 2 Early in the morning He came again into the temple, and all the people were coming to Him; and He sat down and *began* to teach them. 3 The scribes and the Pharisees brought a woman caught in adultery, and having set her in the center *of the court*, 4 they said to Him, "Teacher, this woman has been caught in adultery, in the very act. 5 Now in the Law Moses commanded us to stone such women; what then do You say?" 6 They were saying this, testing Him, so that they might have grounds for accusing Him. But Jesus stooped down and with His finger wrote on the ground. 7 But when they persisted in asking Him, He straightened up, and said to them, "He who is without sin among you, let him *be the* first to throw a stone at her." 8 Again He stooped down and wrote on the ground. 9 When they heard it, they *began* to go out one by one, beginning with the older ones, and He was left alone, and the woman, where she was, in the center *of the court*. 10 Straightening up, Jesus said to her, "Woman, where are they? Did no one condemn you?" 11 She said, "No one, Lord." And Jesus said, "I do not condemn you, either. Go. From now on sin no more."

Dr. John G. Leslie

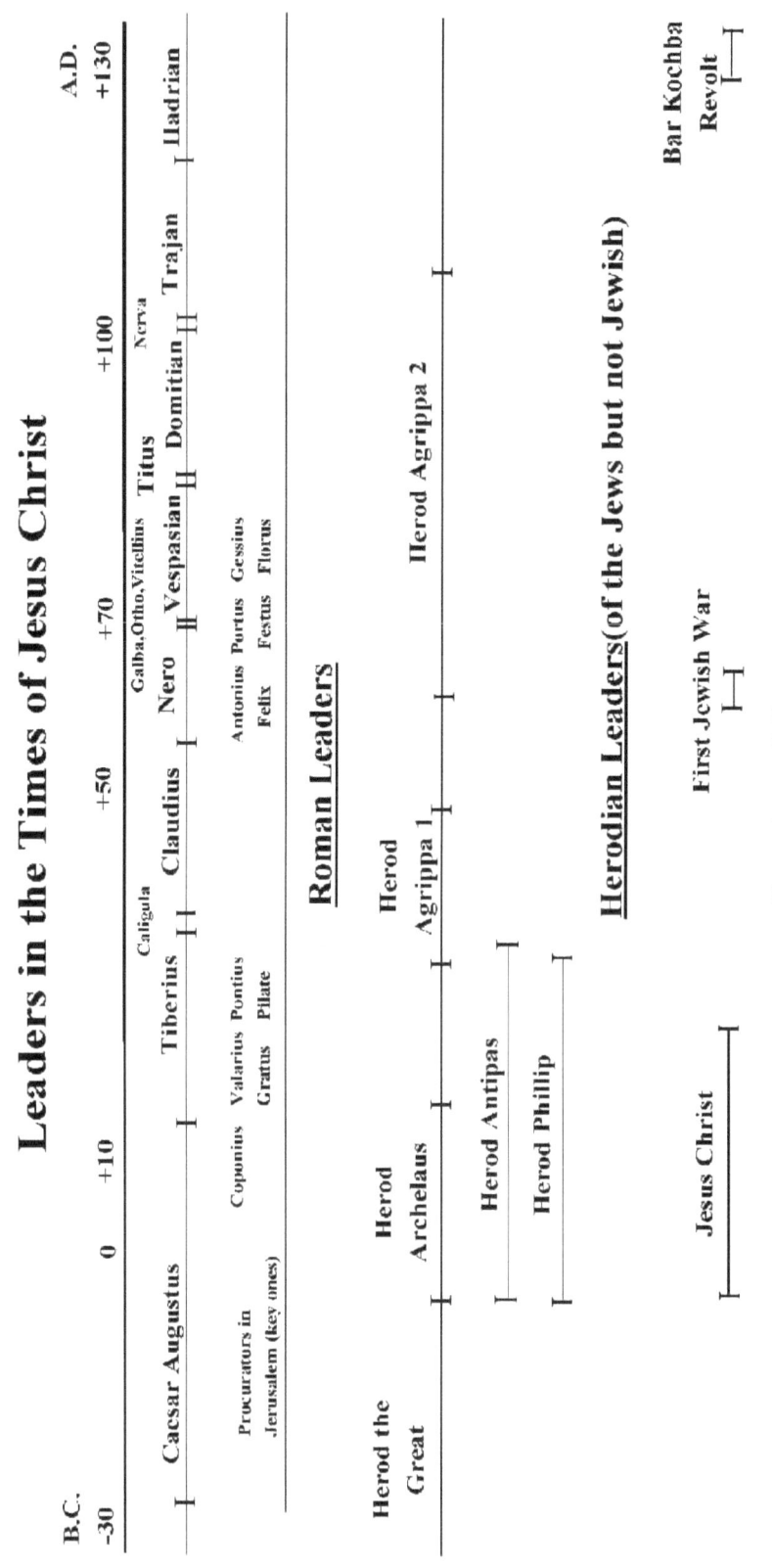

Leaders in the Time of Jesus Christ - Roman Caesars

(See next page for coins.)

1) Augustus: (posthumous stamped by Caligula) He ruled 27 BC-14 AD.

AE[89] Dupondis[90] Obv. DIVVS[91] AVGVSTVS[92] PATER bust left. Rev. SC surrounded by an oak-wreath.

2) Tiberius: He ruled 14 AD-37 AD.

AE Depondis. Obv. TI CAESAR[93] DIVI AVG F AVGVST IMP VIII bust left. Rev. PONTIF MAXIM TRIBVN POTEST XXXVI. (Note: that the ancient peoples may have had a sense of a global shape to the earth as seen that there is a rudder over the globe in this coin.)

3) Caligula: He ruled 37-41 AD but coin not included in figure.

3) Claudius: He ruled 41-54 AD.

AE Dupondis. Obv. TI CLAVDIVS[94] CAESAR AVG M TRP IMPP bust left. Rev. SC with Minerva standing right, brandishing a spear and holding a shield.

4) Nero He ruled Caesar 50-54 AD, Augustus 54-68 AD.

AE Dupondis. Obv. IMP NERO CAESAR AVG P MAX TRPP bust right. Rev. Victory flying left holding a shield inscribed SPQR.

5) Vespasian: He ruled 69-79 AD.

AE As Obv. Aequitas[95] holding scales and scepter. Rev. AEQVITAS AVGST SC.

Augustus Bust (at Glyptothek Munich Public Domain by Bibi Saint-Pol Wikipedia 1-14-15)

---

[89] AE=bronze
[90] A dupondis is worth ½ Sestertius or 1/8 denarius. Wikipedia 7-2016, though it spells it as dupondius but van Meter as dupondis pg75.
[91] DIVO or DIVA means "god". Van Meter pg. 42.
[92] AVGVSTVS or AVG means Augustus. Ibid.
[93] TI CAESAR means Tiberius. Ibid pg. 46.
[94] TI CLAVDIVS means Claudius. Ibid.
[95] "*Aequitas* (genitive *aequitatis*) is the Latin concept of justice, equality, conformity, symmetry, or fairness. It is the origin of the English word 'equity'". Wikipedia for Aequitas online 7-7-2015.

Roman Procurators of Israel

1) Coponius: He ruled 6-9 AD under Augustus.

AE Obv. Barley branch with inscription in Greek KAICA POC (Caesar). Rev. Palm tree with eight branches, two bunches of dates and date LAS (year 36 struck 6 AD). See Hendin 1987 #100 pg. 83.

2) Marcus Ambibulus: He ruled 9-12 AD under Augustus.

Obv. Barley branch with inscription KAICA POC. Rev. Palm tree with eight branches, two bunches of dates and date LAθ (year 39 struck 9AD). Hendin 1987 #102 pg. 83.

3) Valerius Gratus: He ruled 15-26 AD under Tiberius.

Obv. Inscription in Greek IOYΛIA (Julia-mother of Tiberius) within a wreath. Rev. Palm tree flanked by a date LB (year 2 struck 15 AD). Hendin 1987 #105 pg. 84.

4) Pontius Pilate: He ruled 26-36 AD under Tiberius.

Obv. Three bound ears of barley and Greek inscription IOYΛIA KAICA POC. Rev. Libation ladle (simpulum) with inscription TIBEPIOY KAICA POC (of Tiberius Caesar). Date LIS (year 16 struck 29 AD). Hendin 1987 #113 pg. 86.

5) Antonius Felix: He ruled 52-59 AD under Nero.

Obv. Two oblong crossed shields with Greek inscription NEPW KΛAC KAICAP (Nero Claudius Caesar of Claudius). Rev. Six branched palm tree with dates. Greek inscription BPIT (Brittanius second son of Claudius). Date LIΛ KAI (year 14 struck 54 AD). Hendin 1987 #117 pg 87.

6) Porcius Festus: He ruled 59-62 AD under Nero. Obv. Greek inscription within a wreath NEP WNO C (Nero). Rev. Palm branch with Greek inscription KAIC APOC (Caesar). Date LE (year 5 struck in 58 AD). Hendin 1987 # 118 pg. 88.

Leaders in the Times of Christ-Coins

Roman Caesars

Augustus   **Tiberius**   **Claudius**   **Nero**   **Vespasian**

Roman Procurators of Israel

Coponius   **Ambibulus**   **Gratis**   **Pilate**   **Felix**   **Festus**

The Herods

Coins Used in the Teachings of Jesus Christ

1) Widow's Mite

Jesus refers to the faith and commitment of a poor widow in her contribution to the Temple of two of the smallest bronze coins available, which were all she had, as being greater in measure than that of what the rich could give as a fraction of their resources. She gave two lepta (Luke 21:2). In another story reference is made to a man having been forgiven a great amount, and then harshly treating another who owed him only a scant amount of what the previous man had been forgiven. When the ruler who had forgiven the first man found this out the unforgiving man was required to pay all that he had owed even the smallest amount (or lepta). The analogy was that if God has forgiven us, how much more should we forgive each other (Luke 12:59).

2) Tribute Denarius

In responding to a trap set by the Pharisees regarding the use of one's money, Jesus used the silver coin with the image of Caesar to teach on one's obligation to God and to the appointed earthly government. Tiberius was Caesar at the time of Christ's instructions. Jesus said, "render unto Caesar the things that are Caesar's and unto God the things that are God's" (Matthew 22:21). This particular coin was probably made into a charm.

3) Tyre Shekel

The Tyre shekel, called a tetra drachma (four drachma), was produced in Tyre and then in Northern Israel from 183 BC to 69 AD. It was the only accepted silver coin according to the Mishnah for the yearly Temple tax. This was because of its fine accuracy and purity. A 1/2 shekel was required for each male over the age of 18 years old. If one did not have an exact half shekel then exchanges of money were required. This is where the moneychangers made significant amounts of money and which drew Jesus' anger with them. This coin reflected the secular attitudes of the Jewish leaders of that day. The image on the face of the coin was Melchart who was a derivative of Molech. Molech was one of the gods that the children of Israel were to reject and have nothing to do with as part of the worship required child sacrifice. The Jewish leaders were well aware of this issue.

Use of Coins in the Teachings of Christ

Widow's Mite

Tribute Denarius

Tyre Shekel and Half Shekel

(Note: coins are not to scale)

The First Jewish War - (66-70 AD)

Events Leading to the War:

Issues that brought the Jewish people to a "boiling point" of rebellion involved a number of issues. Some were simply economic problems. Examples include increasing taxation by Rome, and inequality among the rich and poor of the Jewish society.[96] The Hasmonean princes had lived lavish lives and the Herodians as well.

It was purported by some that the economic unrest was even stirred up on purpose by some of the Roman procurators for their own self interests. Chief among these was Gessius Florus.[97] The claim was that he was deceitful, corrupt, even robbing the Temple and other illegal gains.[98] It was felt he incited the Jews to anger so as to cover his own actions and could then go to higher authorities in the Roman government to appeal for more restraint. Thus, any legitimate arguments that the Jews might present would be rendered useless.[99] [100]

As well, there had been and was a general disaffection for the Jewish people by the Romans. It centered around the Jewish belief that there was only one true God and that they would not accept the pantheon of Roman and Greek gods as other cultures had.[101] The Jews chose to worship their God in only one place, Jerusalem. Through the long years of struggles regarding the Jewish worship in God they had undergone 5 major assaults of the city by foreign powers.[102] Usually the secular leader desired to put a statue of his favorite god on the Temple Mount area. Jewish Law had forbade any sort of graven image and this too was an affront to the Jews. Caligula (Caesar from 41-37 BC) demanded worship of himself as a deity and ordered a Roman statue placed in the Jewish Temple but he died before it could be done.[103] Procurators such as Florus kept the High Priest garments locked up so that they could not officiate. Jewish people were often denied opportunity to worship in the Temple.

Many of the pagan groups of peoples would attack the Jewish population, and the Roman army would not do anything. The Jews "felt humbled" and that the "Romans were tactless".[104] One Roman historian reported that Tiberius called upon the Jewish people to renounce their faith.[105] The Jews responded with the statement that no sacrifice in the Temple area would be accepted from non-Jewish peoples. Josephus stated that this attitude provoked the Romans and was the issue that began the War. Jewish rebels would begin guerrilla warfare.[106]

---

[96] Grayzel pg. 139.
[97] Wars of the Jews (WOJ) by Josephus book II, chap. 14:1-2.
[98] Ibid Jospehus stated, "But Gessius did his unjust actions to harm the nation after a pompons mannerand as though he had been set up as an executioner to punish condemned malefactors; he omitted no sort of rapine, or of vexation; where the case was really pitiable, he was the most barbarous, and in things of the greatest turpitude he was most impudent. Nor could anyone out do him in disguising the truth; he spoiled whole cities, and ruined entire bodies of men…(gave) liberty to the robbers…(that if) he might go shares in the spoils."
[99] Ibid 15:3
[100] Ibid 16:1
[101] Tacitus Book IV. In general his comments about the Jews were very unflattering. He called them a "superstitious people." He said, "…so sunk in superstition are the Jews and so opposed to all religious practices that they think it wicked to expiate these by sacrifices or vows…even in defeat could not convince them of the truth."
[102] Josephus summarized at the end of book VI (see following pages.)
[103] Josephus WOJ Book 2, chapter 10 (whole chapter).
[104] Grayzel pg. 155.
[105] Suetonius in the Twelve Caesars, chapter on Tiberius, pg 84. "He abolished foreign cults in Rome, particularly Egyptian and Jewish, forcing all citizens who had embraced their superstitions to burn their religious vestments and other accessories…"
[106] WOJ 17:2-3.

Herod Agrippa 2 warned the Jewish people not to go to war and had stated "you will therefore prevent any occasion of revolt if you will but join these together again (talking about the cloister of the Temple with the citadel, the separation making the Temple more of a fortress) and if you will but pay your tribute."[107] The Jewish leaders of the rebellion refused, and in the coming battles Agrippa would actually supply troops to the Roman general Vespasian.[108]

The War:

Initially, Rome would send troops from Syria, the 12th Legion, under Cestius Gallus. They would be ambushed and routed in 66 AD.[109] Josephus, age 29 and without much experience, would be put in charge of the Jewish troops during this time. He did not train the Jewish troops well.[110] In contrast, Nero would select one of his best generals, Vespasian, who would begin to train three legions, up to 60,000 men.[111]

Vespasian would begin his assault of the Jewish lands in 66-67 AD, coming from Syria and first into Galilee.[112] He burnt town/cities to the ground, a "scorched earth" policy, unless the cities surrendered (such as Sepphoris).[113]

Josephus, considered a traitor, left the Jewish forces sometime in 68 AD. He was found by a woman hiding in a well, was turned over to the Romans, and put in prison. He later was released and assisted the Romans (and wrote his Histories of the Jewish People).[114] Galilee would fall to Rome and would be a great loss to the Jewish peoples. Many would begin to flee from the land at this time. Next, Jerusalem would begin to be surrounded, but Vespasian would be called back to Rome to become Caesar. His son, a capable general, would take his place in the land of Judea.[115] Titus then made a decision to breach the walls and not to starve the surrounded peoples in Jerusalem. He used battering rams but met resistance and temporary failure, but then burned the gates. Many more Jews left during this time.[116]

Once the gates were breached and the inner and outer walls, hundreds of thousands of Jewish men, women, and children were taken and sent as slaves, many to the mines. The utensils of the Temple, including the menorah, and lamp stand and other items were captured and paraded through Rome.[117] The Arch of Titus, still in Rome, would be a lasting reminder of this event. The Temple fell in 70 AD, and was burned, but who burned it is controversial.

Once Jerusalem fell, the surviving Jewish fighters (Sicarii) retreated to Masada, a previous Herodean palace on the northeast corner of the Dead Sea. The Romans would build an earthen siege ramp, still visible today, and breach the walls in 74 AD. When they entered the fortress, all the fighters and their

---

[107] WOJ BK II:16:5. It should be remembered that Agrippa II had been raised in Rome.
[108] WOJ BKII:17:4.
[109] Grayzel pg. 163; and WOJ Bk II:19:9.
[110] Grayzel pg. 164.
[111] WOJ BK III:1.
[112] WOJ BK III:2-3.
[113] WOJ BK III:7. Regarding Gadara, "He (Vespasian) came then into and slew all the youth, the Romans having no mercy on any age whatsoever and this was done out of hatred they bore the nation."
[114] WOJ BK III:7:15-18; 8:1-3.
[115] WOJ BK IV:2.
[116] As they leave many of them are massacred by the non-Jewish surrounding population-thinking to get gold from them. WOJ BK IV:8:1-4."So multitudes of Arabians with Syrians cut up those that came as supplicants and searched their bellies…two thousand deserters were thus dissected." Per Josephus Titus was appalled. (8:5)
[117] WOJ BK VI:6:1-4.

families lay dead by suicide except two women and five children.[118]

The Conclusion of the War

From this point on the Jewish people would be dispersed into all the lands of the earth. Coins called "Judea Capta" would be stamped to celebrate the costly victory. This would not be the end of the conflict between the Roman government and the Jewish people. Many self-proclaimed messiahs would appear. Most were apprehended and executed but one would arise that would again stir the people to battle (see Bar Kochba Revolt).

Sadly, it should be noted that during this great contest there were serious conflicts among the Jewish leaders themselves. The three leaders in Jerusalem during the siege were attacking each other, burning each other's supplies and thus severely weakening the resistance by the Jewish rebellion.[119]

Jesus foresaw all these things (Matt. 23:11-39)

[11] But the greatest among you shall be your servant. [12] Whoever exalts himself shall be humbled; and whoever humbles himself shall be exalted. ... [29] "Woe to you, scribes and Pharisees, hypocrites! For you build the tombs of the prophets and adorn the monuments of the righteous, [30] and say, 'If we had been *living* in the days of our fathers, we would not have been partners with them in *shedding* the blood of the prophets.' [31] So you testify against yourselves, that you are sons of those who murdered the prophets. [32] Fill up, then, the measure *of the guilt* of your fathers. [33] You serpents, you brood of vipers, how will you escape the sentence of hell? [34] "Therefore, behold, I am sending you prophets and wise men and scribes; some of them you will kill and crucify, and some of them you will scourge in your synagogues, and persecute from city to city, [35] so that upon you may fall *the guilt of* all the righteous blood shed on earth, from the blood of righteous Abel to the blood of Zechariah, the son of Berechiah, whom you murdered between the temple and the altar.[36] Truly I say to you, all these things will come upon this generation. [37] **"Jerusalem, Jerusalem, who kills the prophets and stones those who are sent to her! How often I wanted to gather your children together, the way a hen gathers her chicks under her wings, and you were unwilling.** [38] Behold, your house is being left to you desolate! [39] For I say to you, from now on you will not see Me until you say, 'BLESSED IS HE WHO COMES IN THE NAME OF THE LORD!'"

---

[118] WOJ BK 7:9:1-2.
[119] WOJ BK IV:3-6;9 and BK II:1, 21,22.

Sacking Of Jerusalem By Rome 70 AD

Upper: Sacking of Jerusalem by David Roberts Lithograph from the original dated 1850 from Wikipedia 9-2015; Lower: Arch of Titus section with menorah. From Wikipedia Arch of Titus by Beth Hatefutsoth CC-by-3.0

Coins of the Jewish War of 66-70 AD

These types of coins stamped in 66-70 AD reflected the Jews' rejection of Roman law, and were consistent with conservative Jewish beliefs regarding Temple images: obverse-amphora, holds liquids such as the wine or oil for the Temple service; reverse- grape leaf, libation of wine on the altar, no human figures. The Temple was destroyed in 70 AD. These types of coins were found at Masada which was overcome in 73-74 AD. (See **Appendices**). Only silver coins were produced during year 1 (and throughout the war) with the exception of one bronze coin (very rare) that was similar to year 2 coins, but with a different arrangement of the lettering in respect to the amphora. Year 2 bronze coins (Prutah) had the amphora with lettering indicating the year. There were several styles of amphora and 2 are shown. A grape leaf is on the back with an inscription in Hebrew designating "Freedom of Zion." Third year coins are somewhat similar but the 4th year bronze coins are different. Hendin 2001, #119, pg. 92.

1) **Jewish War Year 1** silver shekel **Obv**. Omer cup with smooth rim, perals on sides, date above "Year One" and Inscription "Shekel of Israel". **Rev**. Stem with 3 pomegranates. Inscription in Hebrew "Jerusalem the Holy". Border of dots.

2) **Jewish War Year 2** bronze **Obv**. Amphora with broad rim and two handles. Inscription in Hebrew "Year two". **Rev**. Vine leaf with branch/tendrils. Inscription "Freedom of Zion". Hendin 2001 #123, pg. 92; Meshorer #196, pg 241, 338.

3) **Jewish War Year 3** bronze **Obv**. Amphora with broad brim peaked, two handles, and a lid. Inscription "Year Three". **Rev**. Vine leaf on small branch/tendrils. Inscription in Hebrew "Freedom of Zion". Hendin 2001, #126, pg. 95.

4) **Jewish War Year 4** bronze **Obv**. Cup of the Omer (?). Inscription Hebrew "For the Freedom of Zion". **Rev**. Bundle of lulav between two ethrogs. Inscription in Hebrew "Year Four". Dated 70 AD. Meshorer #214a, pg. 243 and 339. Note: Ethrog is a fruit yellowish in color and the lulav which is an unopened palm branch-but it must be just splitting. These are used in the Feast of Sukkot. Hendin 2001 #214a, pg. 243, 339. "And you shall take on the first day the fruit of beautiful trees, branches of palm trees and boughs of leafy trees and willows of the brook, and you shall rejoice before the Lord your God 7 days!" Leviticus 23:40

Jewish War 66-70 AD (Great Revolt)

Year One

(coin photo permit artancient.com)

Year Two

Year Three

Year Four

Judea Capta Coins

"**Judaea Capta** coins… were a series of commemorative coins originally issued by the Roman Emperor Vespasian to celebrate the capture of Judaea and the destruction of the Jewish Second Temple by his son Titus in 70 AD during the First Jewish Revolt…The Judaea Capta coins were struck for 25 years under Vespasian and his two sons who succeeded him as Emperor - Titus and Domitian." From: Wikipedia.

1) Vespasian: Obv. Inscription Latin CAESAR VESPASIANVS AVG (or Imperator Caesar Vespasian Augustus). **Rev**. Jew seated morning below a trophy. Inscription IVDAEA (Judea). Date 69-70 AD. Hendin 2001, #199, pg.120.

2) Titus: (at Caesarea) **Obv**. Head of Titus to right with laureate and inscription in Greek AVTOKP TIT ΟΣ ΚΑΙΣΑΡ. **Rev**. Nike resting with foot on helmet, writing on a shield, and a palm tree. Inscription ΙΟΥΔ ΑΙΑΣ ΕΑΔΛΚΥΙΑΣ (for Judea Capta). Bronze 6.80 gm. Meshorer 2001, #382d, pg 190, 265, 355.

3) Titus (mint at Caesaria) **Obv**. Head of Titus to right with laureate and inscription in Greek AVTOKP ΤΙΤΟΣ ΚΑΙCΑΡ. Rev. Trophy with arms and shields and Jew at base on ground mourning with hands tied behind back, and shield on other side. Rev. Inscription ΙΟΥΑΙΑΣΕΑΛWΚΥΙΑΣ. Date 70 AD. Bronze 13.43 gm. Hendin 2001, #745, pg. 316. Meshorer 2001, #384, pg 190, 265, 355. Possibly minted By Agrippa II.

4) Domitian: Obv. Laureate bust Domitian right draped and Inscription ΛOMET KAI ΓΕΡΜΑΝ. **Rev**. Nike right with foot on helmet, writing on shield and date across field. Inscription ΕΤΟ ΚΛ ΒΑ ΑΓΡΙΙΓΙΓ. Hendin 2001, #604, pg. 217. Struck by Agrippa II at probably at Caesarea Maritima.

5) Counterstamps of Legions of Rome (example the 10th Fretensis) Why countermark coins? Hendin comments[120] "It is possible that the countermarking of coins was necessary for the legionary soldiers more as a psychological tool than a fiscal one…the very visible circulation of countermarked coins could also have a devastating psychological effect on the people living in the territory occupied by the legionary force." Two symbols of the Roman 10th Legion were the numeral ten (X) and the boar. The 10th took part in the destruction of Jerusalem in 70 AD, and in the assault of Masada in 73 AD. It was camped on the Mount of Olives during the Jerusalem campaign. It remained in Jerusalem for many years.[121]

---

[120] Hendin 2001, pg 335.
[121] Ibid pg. 340.

Judaea Capta Coins

1  Vespasian struck 69-70 AD.

2  Titus struck possibly 70 AD.

3  Titus at Caesarea struck 70 AD.

4  Agrippa II under Domitian struck 83 AD.

5  Counter stamp of 10th Roman Legion. Coins on left stamp **X** from Sidon; on right coin with **boar** unknown. Struck 68-96 AD.

(coins are not of comparative scale)

Hadrian's Travels: The Roman Empire and Judea

Hadrian traveled through the Roman Empire during his reign as Caesar.[122] The Roman historian Cassius Deo stated that he was in Judea in 130 AD and that he landed at Gaza.[123] From that event onward til his death in 138 AD coins were minted with his image in Gaza. He then went to Jerusalem and renamed it Aelia Capitolinia.[124] Aelia was his family name. As well, he set up a statue of Jupiter (Zeus) in a pagan temple erected on the Temple Mount.[125] He then began to require that offerings be brought to it. This is symbolized in the Travel Sesterius of Judea which has a Jewish woman with children bringing an offering to him, and there is an altar with a bull inbetween them (he is on the left and she on the right.)

Grayzel[126] comments that Trajan, Caesar before Hadrian, had promised the Jewish people that he would rebuild the Jewish Temple. Grayzel, states that Hadrian was "a man of greater pagan culture and therefore of deeper opposition to any but a pagan faith." Others have commented that he may have been desiring to build a common belief system, with many gods, throughout the Empire.[127] Nonetheless, the Jewish people felt a promise had been broken.

Hadrian next forbade circumcision.[128] With his renaming of Jerusalem to Aelia Capitolina, the requried sacrifices to a pagan god on the Temple Mount, and the forbidance of circumcision (required by the Law) the Jewish people began to see him as another Antiochus Epiphanes IV. This would set the groundwork for the Bar Kochba Revolt.

Hadrian's Travel Sesterius for Judea: Obv. HADRIANVS AVG COS III with a Jewish lady on right handing Hadrian on left an offering over an altar with a bull at its base; rev. ADVENTVI AVG IVDAEAE with a bust of Hadrian facing to the right.

---

[122] Van Mater 2000, pg. 115, 125. Hadrian minted coins for his visit in Gaul, Britannia, Danube Frontier, Spain (Hispania) Asia, Bithynia, Phrygia (Asia Minor), Sicilia, Italia, Africa, Alexandria, Thrace, Moesia, Macedonia, and Judea.
[123] Meshorer 2001, pg. 135.
[124] Grayzel pg. 181
[125] Roman History by Cassius Deo Vol. VIII, 12:1 online. Note: Jupiter, chief Roman god or Zeus in Greek.
[126] Grayzel pg. 181.
[127] Wikipedia Hadrian online 6/27/15.
[128] Grayzel pg. 181.

Hadrian Travel Sestertius
ADVENTVI AVG IVDAEA 130 AD

The Bar Kochba Revolt or Second Revolt

Grayzel[129] stated, "As the situation appeared to the Jews in the year 130, they were faced with the choice of perishing in a cowardly fashion or of fighting to the death on the field of battle…they saw no alternative but to fight." He states that Rabbi Akiba ben Joseph, an eighty year old scholar, became the "most influential among the leaders of the day…He had been to Rome and had believed in Rome's promises. But now that Judaism was threatened, he used his prestige and influence to stir up revolt." However he was too old to lead it.

Simeon Bar Kochba would lead the revolt. He had been born in the town of Koziba. "Strong, imaginative and inspiring, he gave promise of becoming a second Judah Maccabee. Akiba was pleased with him. He called him God's anointed, in other words, messiah…"[130] Akiba changed Simeon's name from Bar Koziba to Bar Kochba "son of the star". He gathered thousands, trained them in the mountains, and by 132 AD began a revolt.

The Jewish "rebels" had intial success against the local Roman troops, but Hadrian would send Julius Severus, a trained leader to combat the situation. Grayzel comments "Severus refused to meet the Jews in open battle (because of their superior numbers)…He harrassed the Jews…waited until they divided their forces and then attacked each part separately." He destroyed land, hindered resources from getting to Bar Kochba, and eventually took Jerusalem. Bar Kochba made a last stand in the Town of Bettar, southwest of Jerusalem. "Thousands upon thousands of them exhausted by the siege, fell fighting in and outside of Bettar."[131] Bar Kochba was killed and the Second Revolt (Bar Kochba Revolt) was finished.

Grayzel goes on to comment that Judaism, now no longer a political force, would become "a kingdom not of this earth, a people without physical boundaries, a group who lived not by the strong arm, like Esau, but by the spiritual qualites of Jacob."[132]

---

[129] Grayzel pg. 181.
[130] Grayzel pg. 182.
[131] Grazel pg. 184.
[132] Grayzel pg. 185.

Cave used by Bar Kochba in the Judean Hills During the 2nd Jewish Revolt

Attribution International 4.0 (CC BY 4.0 upgraded from 2.5) by Udi Steinwell On Wikipedia online 7-11-2015

Letters of Simeon Bar Kochba

(They demonstrate that he is in control and can be quite harsh)

"Shimeon bar Kosiba to Yehonathan and to Masabala.
Let all men from Tekoa and other places who are with you, be sent to me without delay. And if you shall not send them, let it be known to you, that you will be punished."

"From Shimeon bar Kosiba to the men of En-gedi.
To Masabala and to Yehonathan bar Bey'ayan, peace!
In comfort you sit, eat and drink from the property of the House of Israel, and care nothing for your brothers."

From: www.livius.org online 7-11-15

Bar Kochba Coins

Year 1: AE small bronze, 18 mm.

Obv. Palm tree with seven branches and dates. Hebrew inscription (Eleazar the priest). Rev. Bunch of grapes with branch and leaves. Hebrew inscription (Year one of the redemption of Israel).[133]

Year 2: AE bronze, 24 mm.

(Year 2 and 3 very similar except for the arrangement of the lettering on the Obv.)

Obv. Palm tree with seven branches and dates. Hebrew inscription (Simon). Rev. Bunch of grapes with leaf. Hebrew inscription (For the freedom of Jerusalem). Lettering on this coin consistent with year 2.[134]

Year 3: AE small bronze, 18 mm.

Obv. Palm tree with seven branches and dates. Hebrew inscription (Simon). Rev. Bunches of grapes with branch and leaf. Hebrew inscription (For the freedom of Jerusalem).[135]

Note: Many Bar Kochba coins were stamped on previous Roman coinage. This occurred especially on the silver ones. Often older Roman Emperors coins were stamped which some feel may reflect the Jewish people donating their "hoard" of saved coins to the cause.[136]

---

[133] Hendin 2001 #681, pg. 286.
[134] SMG 1981 #529, plate 16.
[135] SMG 1981 #588, plate 18 and Hendin 2001 #739, pg. 302.
[136] Hendin 2001 pg. 281-2.

Bar Kochba War
Year 132-135 AD

(Coins not to comparative scale. Year One coin image from David Hendin Amphora Coins with permit to use.)

Bar Kochba Coin Struck over a Roman Tetradrachm

Hendin comments on the over strike of Roman Coins by Bar Kochba, "One would think, as Leo Mildenberg writes in his now-classic book on Bar Kochba coins, that since 'Hadrian had been emperor for fifteen years when the Bar Kochba War began in 132…a considerable portion of the Bar Kochba silver was over struck upon coins of Hadrian.' Mildenberg quickly adds, however, that 'one would be wrong.'"

"In fact, 'issues, imperial or provincial, of the emperors from Nero to Nerva are frequent among the underlying type, those of Trajan are the most ubiquitous, and those of Hadrian rare. Whatever the reasons for this, the fact itself is irrefutable.' Mildenberg concludes, and I agree, that this indicates that the bulk of the coins Bar Kochba had restruck were not captured directly from Roman Legions in the area, but were instead 'gifts, contributions, taxes, rent or war loans from the Jewish population,' thus 'returning the heavily circulated, by and large pre-Hadrianic money to the Jewish peasants whence it had come, but in a new and specifically Jewish guise.'"[137][138]

This particular coin, a Roman tetradrachm, was over struck with an idealized image of the Jewish Temple that had been destroyed 62-63 years before.

Obv. AR Sela The front of the Temple in Jerusalem with the ark and scrolls, idealized. On three sides are inscribed, in Hebrew, Jerusalem.

Rev. Lulav[139] with an etrog[140] on the left side. Inscribed, in Hebrew, Year one of the redemption of Israel.[141]

---

[137] Hendin 2001 pg. 282.
[138] L. Mildenberg The Coinage of the Bar Kochba War. Salzburg: Verlag Saulander, 1984.
[139] Lulav is the closed frond of a date palm tree.
[140] It is a citrus fruit similar to a lemon. It is important in Sukkot. "On the first day, you must take for yourself a fruit of the citron tree, an unopened palm frond (lulav), myrtle branches, and willows [that grow near] the brook. You shall rejoice before God for seven days." Lev. 23:40. Wikipedia 7-14-15.
[141] Hendin 2001 pg. 283; and Mildenberg 172, 1.

Year Three Coin of the Bar Kochba Rebellion Revealing an Image of the Temple

(Probably somewhat idealized and stamped over a Roman coin)

(Photo image with permit from: Artancient.com)

Bar Kochba Coins Displaying Utensils of Worship and Sacrifice

Simon Ben Koziba, called Simon Bar Kochba or son of the morning star e.g. the Messiah by the rabbi Akiva,[142, 143, 144] felt he was anointed by God to deliver the Jewish people from Roman oppression and to re-establish Temple worship. This belief was reflected on many of his stamped coins.[145] Hendin has stated, "Notable designs included the musical instruments used in the Temple services, as well as the sacred vessels used there."[146]

1) Bronze coin with Lyre: Obv. Three stringed Kithara, wreath and name "Shim'on Prince of Israel"; Rev. "For the freedom of Jerusalem". Jerusalem would appear on 3rd yr. coins.[147]

2) Bronze coin with palm tree: Obv. Palm tree with seven branches and various derivatives of Shim'on. On this Shim' (an abbreviation). It is thought by some that the seven branched palm tree represented the seven branched menorah.[148] Rev. Vine on tendril with Hebrew "Year Two of the freedom of Israel.

3) Silver Zuz: Obv. Trumpets, used in Temple worship, surrounded by Hebrew "To the freedom of Jerusalem." Rev. Lyre "Year two of the freedom of Israel."

---

[142] Hendin 2001 pg. 273. However, not all rabbis would agree with Akiva.
[143] **Akiva ben Joseph** (Hebrew: עקיבא בן יוסף; c. 40 – c. 137 CE), widely known as **Rabbi Akiva** (Hebrew: רבי עקיבא), was a tanna of the latter part of the 1st century and the beginning of the 2nd century (3rd tannaitic generation). Rabbi Akiva was a leading contributor to the Mishnah and Midrash Halakha. He is referred to in the Talmud as *Rosh la-Chachamim* (Head of all the Sages). He recognized Bar Kochba as Messiah, and was executed by the Romans in the disastrous aftermath of the Bar Kochba revolt. Wikipedia online 8-31-15.
[144] "On the other hand, it is certain that the name Bar Kochba is only an epithet derived from R. Akiba's application of the verse to Koziba: 'There shall come a star ['kokab'] out of Jacob who shall smite the corners of Moab and destroy all the children of Seth' (Num. xxiv. 17). Eusebius also ('Hist. Eccl.' iv. 6, 2) adds to the name βαρχωχέβας the remark that it signifies 'star,' and so does Syncellus ('Chronographia,' in the 'Script. Byz.' ix. 348), indicating that they knew that the name was only a figurative one." Jewishencylopedia.com online
[145] He utilized Roman coins, filed them off, then stamped the Jewish images on top of these coins. See Handbook of Biblical Numismatics.
[146] Hendin 2001 pg. 275.
[147] Handbook of Biblical Numismatics.
[148] Jewish Virtual Library online under Second Revolt.

Bar Kochba War Coins Displaying Utensils of Worship and Sacrifice

"The **seven branches of the palm tree could well allude to the holy 7-branched Temple Menorah, that was considered too holy to depict on coins** (with the isolated exception of the small bronze Menorah coin issued in the last desperate days of the reign of Antigonus Mattathias). Bar Kochba's given name appears on the palm tree side either in full with his title: Shim'on the Prince of Israel, or without the title: Shim'on, or shortened as Shim'."
http://www.jewishvirtuallibrary.org/jsource/History/SecondRevolt.html

1 Samuel 16:23 "And it came to pass, when the evil spirit from God was upon Saul, that **David took an harp(lyre or instrument that 'twangs"), and played with his hand**: so Saul was refreshed, and was well, and the evil spirit departed from him." KJV

Bronze palm tree from year 2 coin; silver horns and lyre Zuz/denarius from year 2 and bronze lyre from year 3.

Titus' Arch with Jewish Utensils from the Temple removed in 70 AD (image 1871S. Russell Forbes Rambles in Rome, upload from Project Guttenberg-public domain) Also, Silver Zuz coin permit CC BY-SA 3.0 File:Bar Kokhba Coin.jpg Uploaded by Rullakatriina~commonswiki Created: 22 September 2007

Aelia Capitolina

After Rome's victory in the Bar Kochba Revolt, Hadrian permanently dispersed all Jewish people from Jerusalem. It was unlawful for them to even enter the city. Up to 600,000 Jews had been killed during the Revolt, and all men over the age of 14 had been murdered by the Romans.[149] Women and children were sold as slaves. The Romans also lost a large number of men as upward of five legions, including the II Italica, V Macedonia, VI Ferrata, X Fretensis, and XII Fulminata, had been required to quell the revolt.[150] While Jerusalem had probably been renamed Aelia Capitolina in 130 AD[151] coins did not begin to be stamped there till after 135 AD.

The new coin images were offensive to the Jewish people; the bust of the Caesar was placed on many coins. This was a violation of the Jewish commandment to have no graven images on any property. As well, there were foreign temples with foreign gods, such as Tychae and Zeus portrayed on the coins. This process continued up to the 7th century AD. The Romans very purposefully caused a secularization of Jerusalem.

COINS:

1) Hadrian (117-138 AD): Obv. Bust to right with inscription IMP CAES TRA IANO HADRIANO AVG PP. rev. Hadrian plowing a field with an ox and a bull inscription COL AEL KAPIT.

2) Antonius Pius (136-161AD): Obv. Bust to right inscription unreadable. rev. bust of goddess Tychae to right inscription COL AEL CAP.

3) Diadumenian (217-218 AD): Obv. Bust to right inscription M OPEL DIADVMENIANVS C. rev. tetra-style temple with statue of Tychae within it inscription surrounding it COL AEL PF COS.

---

[149] Hendin 1987, pg. 149.
[150] Hendin 2001, pg. 335.
[151] "**AELIA CAPITOLINA**, the city built by the emperor Hadrian, A.D. 131, and occupied by a Roman colony, on the site of Jerusalem (*q.v.*), which was in ruins when he visited his Syrian dominions. *Aelia* is derived from the emperor's family name, and *Capitolina* from that of Jupiter Capitolinus, to whom a temple was built on the site of the Jewish temple." Encycopeadia Britannica 1911 online 8-31-15.

Aelia Capitolina
(Mint in Jerusalem)
Roman Coins Stamped 135-260 AD
(Examples)

Hadrian
117-138 AD
135 AD Jerusalem
renamed as above

Antonius
Pius
138-161 AD

Diadumenian
217-218 AD

(Not to scale)

CHAPTER 8   TIMES OF THE GENTILES: 132 AD TO 1917 AD

132-300 AD: "Until the Bar Kochba revolt, 132-135, the difference between Judaism and Christianity was not clear even to most Jews…But during the revolt it became clear to the Jews that neither Jewish Christians nor Gentile Christians wanted the Jews to win. On the contrary, the Christians were rather anxious to have the Jews defeated since the latter looked upon Bar Kochba as a messiah, and his victory would destroy many Christian claims for Jesus. Some Christians were active against the Jews. As a result the Jews adopted regulations which successfully excluded all Christians from the synagogues and from Jewish life in general. For example, the Jews included in their *Amidah* (the Eighteen Benedictions) a prayer asking for the disappearance of sectarians." Sectarians would have included Christians. On the other hand Greyzel stated that some Christians "even denied the right of the Jewish people to continue to exist."[152] I think this statement a bit harsh but clearly a divide had been created by the Bar Kochba revolt.

300 AD: Constantine (see coin) declared Christianity the official religion of the Roman/Byzantine Empire.[153] It should be noted that up until that proclamation both Jews and Christians had been persecuted in the Roman Empire.

310-636: Byzantine Empire. During this time "…the more ambitious and politically-minded among their leaders (Byzantine ones) began to do everything possible to bring about the humiliation if not the destruction of their Jewish rivals."[154]

361: Julian (The Apostate) persecuted Christians but left the Jewish people alone. He died after two years.[155]

390: The commentary on the Mishna, called the Gamara, was completed. It along with the Mishna made up the Palistinian Talmud.[156] The Babylonian Talmud appeared about 150 years later as a refinement to the Palestinian one.

---

[152] Greyzel pg. 212.
[153] Ibid 213.
[154] Greyzel pg. 213. While I think that this is an overstatement by Grazel, it does reflect an attitude among some so-called believers in Christ. Jesus never talked about dominating others, but loving and laying down one's life in service for them. 1 John 3:16 "Here by perceive we the love of God, because he laid down his life for us: and we ought to lay down our lives for the brethren." Yet, there is a place for government to restrain lawlessness, but that is not the situation here.
[155] Grayzel pg. 215
[156] IMFA pg. 3. And Grayzel pg. 215.

425: The last Patriarch, Gamaliel VI, from the line of Hillel (leading rabbi and born in Babylon) died. Rome then abolished the office in 429. The Patriarchate had been responsible for codifying Jewish Law. Greyzel comments, "During the fifteen hundred years of Jewish life in Palestine there was never a generation which did not produce important books…the books included the Apocrypha, great poetry, novels, dramas and visionary writings…No Jew has ever thought of the end of that era without a pain of regret…there has always been an ardent hope for the re-establishment of Palestine as the homeland of the Jewish people."[157]

470: Rav Ashi, the head scholar among the Babylonian Jews at Susa, refined the Mishna. The Talmud was fully completed. It concentrated on the writings regarding Jewish life in the Diaspora (lands outside of Judea).

200's-500's The Babylonian Jewish community continued to grow, and pursued learning. An Exilarch leadership was developed, but corruption among these leaders weakened the influence of Jews among other peoples.[158]

500-600: Jewish thought continued to penetrate into Arab cultures. And Jews and Christians were called "People of the Book."[159]

224-651: The Sasanid Empire (neo-Persia) ruled Babylon with varying degrees of religious freedom. **Khosrou(w) II** (see coin) ruled from 590-628.[160] He took Jerusalem from the Byzantine Empire during the Sasanid-Byzantine War 602-628. A portion of what was thought to be the "True Cross" and other relicts were taken by Khosrou II back to his capitol at Ctesiphor. But Heraclius, a Byzantine Emperor, took back Jerusalem in 629 AD.[161]

613-632: Islam Muhammed began preaching. He stated that he was God's final prophet, and many Arab people groups accepted him as such.[162] Jesus was relegated to that of one of many other prophets. Anyone who did not accept Islam was lost.[163,164] Mohammed began a series of military operations against those whom opposed him, including gathering 10,000 men to take the city of Medina.[165]

620 Islamic tradition stated that Muhammed ascended to heaven temporarily from Mt Moriah.

632 (or 636)-1099 Arab Rule throughout the Middle East.

---

[157] Grayzel pg.219. He wrote and published his book in 1947, just one year before Israel became a legal nation (in the eyes of the world). This was a fulfillment of prophecy: Ezekiel 11:17 "Therefore say, Thus saith the Lord GOD; I will even gather you from the people, and assemble you out of the countries where ye have been scattered, and I will give you the land of Israel."

[158] Grayzel Chapter VII and pg. 276-77.

[159] Ibid pg. 243-45.

[160] He was the last great Sasanid leader. Muhammad wrote him a letter offering him to accept Islam or face judgment for the sins of those leaders before him.

[161] There would continue to be war over Jerusalem as Jesus Christ prophesied Luke 19:42 "Saying, If thou hadst known, even thou, at least in this thy day, the things which belong unto thy peace! but now they are hid from thine eyes. [43] For the days shall come upon thee, that thine enemies shall cast a trench about thee, and compass thee round, and keep thee in on every side, [44] And shall lay thee even with the ground, and thy children within thee; and they shall not leave in thee one stone upon another; because thou knewest not the time of thy visitation."

[162] Quran 2:136. See also Wikipedia on Mohammed, "Seal of the Prophets" in Sura Al-Ahzab 33:40.

[163] Quran 3:70-79.

[164] In his saying, Jews who do not accept Islam are cursed with the fire of hell. Ibid 4:50. What the practical significance in this teaching of Muhammad's is that the blessing on Isaac (Gen. 17:21) is being transferred to Ishmael. Sura 2:130-32. It would seem that this would be very attractive to many Arabs, yet it would be in contrast to the initial writings of Moses whom Islamic believers say is a prophet.

[165] Wikipedia on Mohammed.

636-37 Caliph Um the Great conquered Jerusalem. Months earlier, the Eastern Byzantine Empire had been defeated at the Battle of Yarmouk.

661-750 The Umayyad Empire: Muawiyah I was ordained Caliph of the Islamic world in Jerusalem. This was the beganning of the Umayyad Empire.[166] This group standardized weights/measures and stamp coins with only verses of the Quran in the countries that they subdued.[167] (see coin)

691 Al-Aqsa Mosque built by Caliph Abd el-Malik on the site of the 1st and 2nd Temple (Mt. Moriah).[168]

600's-700's "…in little less than one hundred years Mohammedanism had spread from the half-forgotten Arabian desert to include lands as far apart as the northern border of India and the Pyrenees south of France. Babylonia, Palestine and Egypt were theirs, the cradles of ancient civilization. These lands began to nourish a new culture, certain to affect the culture of their Jewish inabitants."[169] In areas that Islam had conquered the **Pact of Omar** was put into effect. "Its object was to make it perfectly clear that members of another religious group were inferior to Mohammedans…forbidden to speak disrespectfully of Mohammed…taxation which non-believers had to bear was always to be heavy. No new synagogues…no synagogues (or church) could be higher than a neighboring mosque." Non-belivers had to use donkeys rather than horses, nor could they carry swords. "Kalif Mutawakki, in 850, ordered that non-Moslems be forced to wear a yellow patch on their sleeves as well as a yellow head-dressing."[170] Greyzel did comment that under Muslim rules Jewish communities were allowed to persist and practice their own religion.[171]

732 Charles Martel stopped the advance of Islam into Europe at the Battle of Tours.[172]

750 The Abbasids defeated the Umayyads, and attempted to kill as many of the royal clan as possible to prevent reprisals. Abd al Rahnan escaped to Spain and continued the Umayyad clan there.[173] (see coin)

782 The Abbasids moved the capitol to Bagdad.

---

[166] Jewish Virtual Library.
[167] Portland State University-Middle East Teaching Tools. www.middleeastpdx.org/resources/wp-content/upload/2012/11/Lesson-1-Abbasid-Umayyad-History.pdf.
[168] This has profound implications for prophecy for the Bible states in Micah 4 "But in the last days it shall come to pass, that the mountain of the house of the LORD shall be established in the top of the mountains, and it shall be exalted above the hills; and people shall flow unto it. ² And many nations shall come, and say, Come, and let us go up to the mountain of the LORD, and to the house of the God of Jacob; and he will teach us of his ways, and we will walk in his paths: for the law shall go forth of Zion, and the word of the LORD from Jerusalem." It is my understanding that the Jewish Temple will be re-built in the same area in the "Last Days".
[169] Grayzel pg. 251.
[170] Grayzel pg. 253. This would be a forbearer of Nazi treatment of the Jews in Germany in the 20th Century.
[171] Ibid pg. 253.
[172] "The **Battle of Tours** (October 732), also called the **Battle of Poitiers** and in Arabic: معركة بلاط الشهداء (*ma'arakat Balâṭ ash-Shuhadâ – Battle of the Palace of Martyrs*) was fought in an area between the cities of Poitiers and Tours, in north-central France, near the village of Moussais-la-Bataille, about 20 kilometres (12 mi) northeast of Poitiers. The location of the battle was close to the border between the Frankish realm and then-independent Aquitaine. The battle pitted Frankish and Burgundian forces under Austrasian Mayor of the Palace Charles Martel against an army of the Umayyad Caliphate led by 'Abdul Rahman Al Ghafiqi, Governor-General of al-Andalus." From Wikipedia online 9-8-15.
[173] Portland State University: see previous reference to site.

750-900 This period has been considered the Golden Age of Muslim achievements. "During the reign of the Abbasids Rule 750 AD the Muslim world saw the height of power and glory."[174] In 758 Al-Mansur repaired the Dome of the Rock. He also "ordered the destruction of the crosses on the churches and forbade the Christians to hold services at night."[175] Caliph Harun al-Rashid (786-809) relaxed these edicts.

1095-1270 The Crusades: The first Crusaders, 1096-99, briefly captured Jerusalem and massacred the non-Christian inhabitants, including the Jews.[176] In 1187 Saladin (an Ayyubid) recaptured it, and Jews were allowed back in the city. Seven more Crusades occurred. In the 6th Crusade, 1228-1229, Fredrick II negotiated a treaty which allowed Christians access to Jerusalem and supervision of several holy sites in Judea. Muslim mercenaries retook Jerusalem in 1244.[177]

One Crusader, who was outside of the usual accepted period for the Crusades, but who had a great concern for Jerusalem and the Christians there was **Hethum I** (1215?-1271). He founded a dynasty: the Hetoumids. He then submitted to the Mongol Empire, and even traveled to Mongolia (long before Marco Polo) to visit its king Mongke Khan. He encouraged him to convert to Christianity but he refused.[178] Hethum did send troops to the Mongols to help battle Islamic forces. They initially conquered Damascus, but were then driven back in 1260 at the battle of Ain Jalut.[179] He retired to become a monk.[180] It is not known to this author what his views were regarding the Jewish people. (See coin)

1173-1341 Continued Arab Involvement in Jerusalem:

1173-1250 The Ayyubids: These were "Kurdish soldiers of fortune" with **Saladin** as one of the prominent leaders. He prepared them for war and fought against the Crusaders. He died in 1193. In their evangelistic efforts the Ayyubids set up madrassa, academies of sciences, to attract Jews and Christians to the Muslim faith. They were overcome by the Mamluks in Egypt at the Battle of A-Mansurah.[181] (see coin)

1250-1516 The Mamluks: This group ruled from Egypt into Syria/Palestine during this period. "…local Jews often suffered at the hands of government officials and Muslim zealots, although at times the sultan and his representatives were also a restraining influence on fanatical mobs or leaders. The Mamluks were one of the most important dynasties in the history of medieval Islam, gaining fame for stopping the Mongol advance into Syria and for eradicating the Crusader presence in Palestine and elsewhere along the Syrian coast."[182] For over 250 years it ruled the area first by "Turkish" leaders then by "Circassian" ones. They revived the caliphate. Mamluks were eventually overcome by the Ottoman Empire in 1517-18, but some remained in power in Egypt. Generals from the Mamluk sect rose to power when the Ottomans began to diminish. But Muhammad Ali Pash massacred remaining Mamluk leaders in 1811.[183]

---

[174] One of the leaders: Abbas ibn Abdal-Muttalib was Muhammad's uncle. From: Jerusalem.com.
[175] Archpark.org il/article.asp? Id=235. Also, this man had been in communication with Charlemagne, King of the Franks.
[176] www.jewishvirtuallibrary.org/jsource/History/Crusader.
[177] Ibid pg. 2
[178] Per the reference the king stated that it would be too big a change for his people. From Google online book: Faith Across Time: 5000 Years of Religious History. By Gordon Melton in 4 Volumes. Pg. 845.
[179] Wikipedia: Hethum I online 9/8/2015.
[180] His son too became a monk, and may have traveled to Jerusalem in 1300 AD. Wikipedia Hethoum II.
[181] Brittanica.com/article/46670.
[182] Encyclopedia Judaica: Mamluks, and www.jewishvirtuallibrary.org/jsosurce/judicial/ejud_0002_0013_0_13118
[183] Mamluk in www.Britannica.com/article/360799.

1453-1914(7) The Ottoman Empire: Developed out of Turkey and lasted 600 years. The Ottomans aligned with Germany in WW1 and lost control over Palestine[184] in 1917. The area of Turkey became a republic in 1922.[185] At its height of expansion it covered Hungary, Southeastern Europe, the Balkans, Greece, parts of the Ukraine, Palestine and Egypt, parts of North Africa, and Arabia. (See coin)

It was begun by Osman and "nomadic Turkman" about 1300 AD.[186] Their history was one of violence/conquest/loss/restoration. They had numerous battles with the Byzantine Empire and the Crusaders. The last group they defeated at the Battle of Nicopolis in 1396.[187]

A system of government developed: "The basic class divisions within the subject class were determined by religion, with each important group organizing into a relatively self-contained autonomous religious community usually called a *millet* (also *taife* or *cemaat*), which operated under its own laws and customs and was directed by a religious leader responsible to the sultan for the fulfillment of the duties and responsibilities of the *millet* members, particularly of paying taxes and security."[188] It should be noted that the legal system was based on Shari-ah law (Muslim religious law) and a civil law. Thus, Christians and Jews were under Islamic Law.

The Empire began to degenerate when greed and corruption occurred among the leaders. A group called the *devsirme* began to usurp the sultans. It degraded into the grand visier then the women of the harems "sultanate of the Women", and finally to the Janissary officers (the Agas) in 1578-1625. "…a growing paralysis of administration throughout the empire" occurred.[189] This led to severe economic lack of produce and increased bands of rebels, though the army kept a wholesale revolt from occurring. Conflicts occurred with other nations nearby.[190] Yet, some leaders of the Ottomans still tried to live ostentaciously. During the "so-called Tulip Period (1717-30), some Ottomans under the influence of the grand visier Ibrahim Pasa began to dress like Europeans, and the palace began to imitate European court life and pleasures."[191]

Some reforms did occur so as to build up the military, and a plan for state education (as opposed to the *millets* doing it) was developed in 1846. "By 1914 there were more than 36,00 Ottoman schools…"[192]

Pan-Islamism was promoted by Ottoman leaders starting about 1774 in a treaty with Russia whereby authority was claimed over Muslims in areas outside the Ottoman Empire. It was used as a tool in negotiations with neighboring countries. Conflicts within and without the borders of the Ottoman Empire continued to weaken it during the 1800's and earlier 1900's.

Some felt that the Ottoman entry into WW1 on the side of Germany was hasty in hope of gaining some advantage. At the end of the war in 1916 by the Anglo-Franch Sykes-Picot Agreement Britain was given oversite of Haifa and Akko and Palestine was placed under international control.[193]

---

[184] "As a consequence of the Bar Kochba revolt, in 135 CE the region was renamed and merged with Roman Syria to form *Syria Palaestina* by the victorious Roman Emperor Hadrian."From: Wikipedia on Judea. Prior it had been Judea.
[185] Ottoman Empire: wwwbritannica.com/article/434996.
[186] Ibid. pg.1
[187] Ibid pg.7
[188] Ibid pg.15
[189] Ibid pg.17
[190] Ibid pg.18,19.
[191] Ibid. pg.20
[192] Ibid pg. 24
[193] Ibid pg.30

Kac[194] made some very interesting comments some about Gentile leaders that lived in the 1600's to early 1900's. "The wide diffusion of a knowledge of the Bible brought about by the Protestant Reformation has led to a growing belief among Christian people of the eventual restoration of the Jewish people to Palestine. This belief was especially strong in Great Britain." Lord Palmerston, British Ambassador to Porte wrote in a letter dated August 11, 1840, "There exists at present among the Jews dispersed over Europe a strong notion that the time is approaching their nation is to return to Palestine…" Kac noted that, "Even before the end the seventeenth century at least twelve publications had appeared in England advocating the return of the Jews to Palestine, mainly on religious grounds. In the minds of many Christians this return was looked on as a fulfillment of prophecy, and linked with the Second Coming of Christ." Many humanitarian actions were born out of this belief.

Books listing some prominent leaders were printed. The lists included: Paul Knell 1648, John Milton, Oliver Cromwell, others; and Thomas Brightman who wrote in 1641 in reference to the Jewish people, "What! Shall they return to Jerusalem again? There is nothing more certain: the prophets do everywhere confirm it?" Roger Williams, the founder of Rhode Island, "was an ardent believer in the restoration of Israel."[195] In the 1700's Edward King, William Whiston (scientist), Bishop Robert Lowth of London, Philip Dodridge (religious author), John Scott and others supported the return of the Jews to Israel. Scott in his book The Destiny of Israel, 1813, comments regarding the view of the Jews having been cast off from God, "Have they stumbled that they might fall, to rise no more? God forbid! All the facts we have before us, and particularly their preservation, might well raise hopes in our minds that mercy was still in reserve for Israel!" John Adams, second President of the US, "in a letter to Major Mordecai Maneul said, 'I really wish the Jews again in Judea, an independent nation…'" Lord Byron and George Eliot were also sensitive to the Jewish people.

In the 1800's Lord Shaftesbury, A.G.H. Hollingsworth, Thomas Clarke, James Finn, Laurence Oliphant and others supported the return of the Jews to Israel.

In the late 1800's to early 1900's Kac commented: "Of men like Balfour, Lloyd George, Churchill, Lord Milner, and General Smuts, Weizmann says that they 'were deeply religious, and believed in the Bible, that to them the return of the Jewish people to Palestine was a reality, so that we Zionists represented to them a great tradition for which they had enormous respect…Those British statesmen of the old school, I have said, were genuinely religious.They understood as a reality the concept of the Return (the return of the Jews to Zion). It appealed to their tradition and their faith."[196]

---

[194] The Rebirth of the State of Israel by Arthur Kac, copyright 1958 by Marshal, Morgan and Sons Ltd., and printed By Moody Press, Chicago, Il.
[195] Ibid pg. 49-50.
[196] Ibid 50-51.

24. Second Assault of Jerusalem: The Crusaders Repulsed
The Crusaders leave the battlefield disappointed after twelve hours of fighting.

(From Gustave Dore Public Domain)

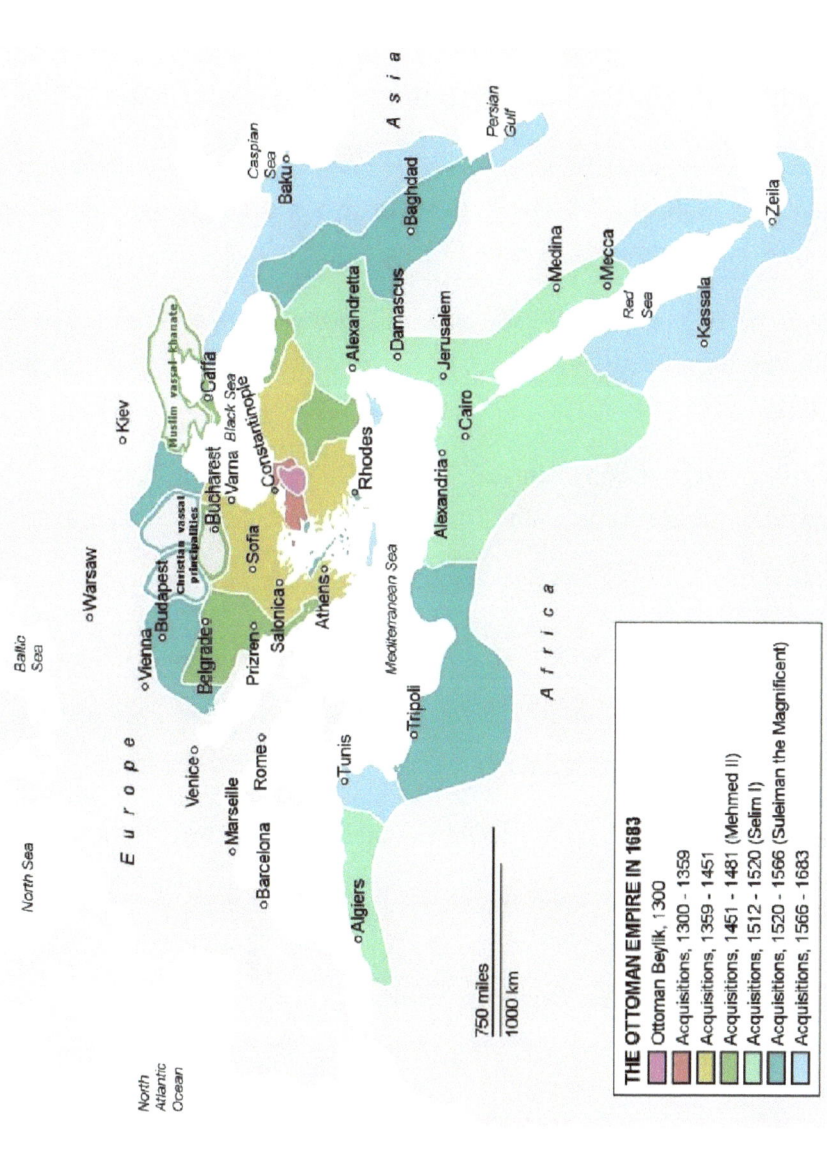

Atilim Gunes Baydin - Self drawn, mainly based on Robert Mantran (ed.), Histoire de l'Empire Ottoman, Paris: Fayard (1989), also en:List of Ottoman Empire dominated territories, Image:Ottoman 1683.Public Domain Wikipedia online 9-8-15

Examples of Leaders on Coins during the Period

1. Roman Period 4 BC-299 AD: Tiberius Obv. Tiberius face to left with Ti Caesar divi avg F. Rev. Pontiff Maxim Tribvn XXXVI, rudder superimposed on globe. Van Mater Tiberius 317 pg. 76, 1991. He ruled from 14 AD-37 AD. Many coins had "divi" which implied divinity and involved emperor worship.

2. Late Roman Period 300 AD: The Era of Constantine. Coin of Constantius II 348 AD. Obv. Head with diad. Rev. Fel Temp Reparatio with Emperor dragging captive by hair.

3. Byzantine 300-1453 AD: Basil II (976-1025). Obv. Bust of Christ facing and holding book of gospels. Rev. ihsys/xristys basiley basile (probably) Sear 1818.

4. Sasanian Period 225-651 AD: Khusro II (580-628 AD). Obv. Winged crown with 3 melons, 3 short diadems and ties behind, crescent with star above. Rev. Two attendants flanking a burning altar, 4 crescents with stars at opposite sides-symbolic of Zoroastrianism.

5. Umayyad Period 661-750 AD: Anonymous (695-750). Obv. Possible Menorah. Rev. "Aliya, Madinet Bayit al-Maqdis" in Arabic means Aelia Capitolina a Roman name for Jerusalem.

6. Abbassid Period 750-1517 (or 1258) AD: Abbasid Caliphate Al Mansur (753-774 AD). Fals.

7. Ayyubid 1174-1341 AD: Possibly Saladin (1174-1193 AD); or Al-Zahir Ghazi (1206-1215 AD).

8. Crusaders 1095-1270 AD: Example Hethum I (ruler 1226-1271 AD). Obv. King on throne. Rev. Potent cross with Armenian legend around it.

9. Mamluk 1250-1517: Possibly Baybars I, 1260-1277 AD. He inadvertently drank poisoned wine. (Encyclopedia Britannica online.)

10. Ottoman 1453-1918 AD: Probably Sultan Bayezid (1389-1402 AD). Silver Akce. www.ancientresource.com/lots/islamic-arabic/ottoman.

Times of the Gentiles Til 1917

Roman Period (Time of Christ) 4 BC-299 AD   **Late Roman 300 AD** Constantine

Byzantine 300-1453 AD   **Sasanian 224-651 AD** Khusro 2

Umayyad 661-750 AD   **Abbasid 750-1517AD**

Ayyubid 1174-1341 Saladin   **Crusades 1095-1272 AD** Hethoum 1 Armenia

Mamluk 1250-1517 AD   **Ottoman 1453-1917 AD**

(Coins not to relative scale)

CHAPTER 9   TIMES OF THE GENTILES FROM 1904/17 TO 1947/48

The name of Palestine is thought to have been derived "from the Egyptian and Hebrew word 'peleshet,' roughly translated to mean 'rolling' or 'migratory'."[197] It is applied to the area where the Philistines were found, probably related to the Greeks (and not Arabs).[198] The term "Palestine" was used by the Greek historian Herodotus in 400 BC and by the Romans after the Bar Kochba War. During the Ottoman period the area was connoted either 'Palestine" or "Southern Syria.' And "after WWI the name 'Palestine' was applied to the territory that was placed under British Mandate." It included both present day Israel and Jordan.[199]

The Israel Ministry of Foreign Affairs (IMFA) has on their website a timeline for this period of history.[200] This is used below with comments from other sources as well:

1904-1914
A significant influx of Jews occurred to England and France from Eastern Europe.[201] Second Aliya:[202] the name of this movement to Judea. Tel Aviv was founded.

1917
The Ottoman Empire rule in Judea was removed; Gen. Allenby was in Jerusalem. Balfour Accord reflected English support for establishment of a "Jewish National Home."[203]

1914-1918
In 1917 the Jewish Welfare Board was set up in the United States to help Jewish families during WWI. And even with Germany's anti-Semitic laws about 100,000 Jewish soldiers fought for it. One third of the soldiers were decorated for bravery. Jews were also soldiers in France and England. It was common for Russian Jews to fight for their adopted countries.[204]

---

[197] Virtualjewishlibrary.com online 8-2015.
[198] Greyzel comments on pg. 33 "The little province of Judea, too, was at rest in the general drowsiness. It was one of the least important of Persia's subject states. It sent no caravans on the highways of commerce…consequently no one heard of the Jews. The Greeks, who were at that time the only people interested in history, philosophy and geography, **called the land between the Mediterranean and the Jordan 'Philistia'(Palestine), because the only people they knew in that land were the Philistines who lived on the coast**…The Greeks who enshrined their many capricious gods and goddesses on Mount Olympus, were astounded to find a people who thought that it a sin to make a statue of their God, who turned heavenward in prayer, and who considered their God's chief interest to be justice and righteousness."
[199] Virtualjewishlibrary.com online 8-2015.
[200] http://mfa.gov.il/MFA/AboutIsrael/History/Pages/Facts%20about%20Israel-%20History.aspx
[201] In Germany: "The Jews were pained by the government's disregard of their constitutional rights…practical impossibility of a Jew obtaining a professorship…commission in the army." Grayzel pg. 707. Russian Pogroms: …"the massacre in Kishine at Easter 1903 saw dozens killed…" pg. 709.
[202] "**Aliyah** (UK /ˈælɪˈɑː/, US /ˌɑːliˈɑː/; **Hebrew**: עֲלִיָּה **aliyah**, 'ascent') is the immigration of Jews from the diaspora to the land of **Israel** (Eretz Yisrael). Also defined as 'the act of going up' or as in progressing towards Jerusalem, **Aliyah** is one of the most basic tenets of Zionism." From: Wikipedia online 9-3-15.
[203] IMFA pg. 3 Note also that IMFA spells aliya not aliyah.
[204] Grayzel pg. 712.

1919-1921
"Over twelve hundred pogroms[205] occurred in the Ukraine alone… (also) in Poland, Hungary, Rumania and elsewhere."[206]

1922
Britain was granted Mandate by the League of Nations. Land mass ¾ Trans-Jordan and ¼ "Jewish National Home."[207] The Legal Instrument: British Mandate for Palestine. This included both of what would become "Palestine" and "Trans-Jordan".

Walter Rathenau, a German industrialist and Jew, was involved in the post war recovery of Germany. He was assassinated by an anti-Semitic German group in 1922. As a result France re-occupied a part of Germany, which was said to have increased anti-Semitic hostility there.[208]

1919-1923
3rd Aliya mainly from Russia occurred.[209] Haganah (self defense, who prepare for war) and Irgun (who actively fight British and Arabs) were formed.[210] Hebrew Dictionary was completed by Eliezer ben Yehudah. Recurring conflict occurred between Arab and Jewish populations.[211]

1924-1932
4th Aliya mainly from Poland occurred.[212]

1924
Technical Institute of Technology-Haifa was started.

1925
Hebrew University opened on Mt Scopus.[213]

1929
The Hebron massacre occurred among Jews in a conflict with Arabs.[214]

1933
The Nationalist Socialist Party (Nazis) gained control in Germany. Hitler promoted the idea of the extermination of the Jewish people.

1936-1939
Increased anti-Jewish riots in Germany and elsewhere. 5th Aliya occurred mainly from Germany.

---

[205] Pogroms "A **pogrom** is a violent riot aimed at massacre or persecution of an ethnic or religious group, particularly one aimed at Jews. The term originally entered the English language to describe 19th- and 20th-century attacks on Jews in the Russian Empire (mostly within the Pale of Settlement in present-day Ukraine and Belarus)." Wikipedia online 9-3-15.
[206] Grayzel pg. 714.
[207] IMFA pg. 3.
[208] Grayzel pg. 726.
[209] Ibid.
[210] Grayzel pg. 706.
[211] Grayzel pg. 724.
[212] Remember the movie "Fiddler on the Roof."
[213] The cornerstone had been laid on 7/24/15 at the spot where Titus had ordered the destruction of Jerusalem in 69 AD. Grayzel pg. 718.
[214] IMFA pg. 3.

1939

Jewish immigration was limited to Palestine by British White Paper.

1939-1945   WW2 Holocaust.

1942

Warsaw ghetto population went from 3 million to 0.2 million Jews during the war. Germany 0.5 million to less than 100 people. (A reduction of 99.8% from beginning to end of the war.) Holland 0.15 million to 0.03, Czechoslovakia 0.36 million to 0.05 million. During WW2 approximately 6 million Jews were killed (about 1/3 of all Jews, and ½ of European Jews).[215]

1946

Trans-Jordan was separated from Palestine and Hashemite authority and sovereignty accorded to its leader Abdullah Hussein.[216]

1947

United Nations (superseding the League of Nations) proposed to establish Arab and Jewish states in what is now called Palestine.[217] The Arab League voted against any partition.[218, 219]

1948 May 14   British Mandate was ended.

1948 May 14   State of Israel began. It was supported by President Truman.[220]

1948 May 15   Israel was invaded by five Arab nations.[221]. Egypt bombed Tell Aviv on that day.[222] England refused to sell arms to Israel, but Czechoslovakia did.[223]

1949

An Armistice was signed between Egypt (2/24), Lebanon (3/23), Jordan/Iraq (4/3), and Syria (4/20).[224] Jerusalem was divided and Jordan and Israel each supervised one half. The Temple Mount today remains under Islamic supervision.[225]

---

[215] Grayzel pg. 789-90. He wrote his book in 1948. He did comment that many Christians did help Jewish People.

[216] Wikipedia "British Mandate for Palestine" online 9-2015.pg 11.

[217] Many Jewish people feel that Trans-Jordan should still be a part of Israel. Simcha Jacobovici complained in an article he wrote regarding the term Palestine in 2013; "The area of Palestine never became an independent state. In the 7th century, Muslim armies conquered it, precipitating battles with Christian crusaders for the "Holy Land". These bloody battles are now remembered as the 'Crusades". In modern times, the province of Palestine passed from the Ottoman Turks to the British. In 1922, the British gifted a chunk of Palestine to the Hashemite clan from Saudi Arabia. In 1946, 80% of British mandate Palestine-the area east of the Jordan River-became the modern Hashmite Kingdom of Jordan. One year later, 20% of British controlled Palestine became what is today the State of Israel and the Palestinian territories." The Times Of Israel at: blogs.timesofisrael.com/palistine-history-of-a-name/. He clarifies that the term Palestine was not given to the area till after the Bar Kochba War in 135 AD, by the Romans to remove any history of the Jewish people living in what before then had been called Judea or Israel. It should be noted that even Jerusalem was then re-named Aelia Capitolina by Hadrian.

[218] Israel by Martin Gilbert, 1998 with addendums 2008, pg. 141.

[219] Ibid, pg. 153-4. Moshe Dyan stated, "I felt in my bones the victory of Judaism, which for two thousand years of exile from the Land of Israel had withstood persecutions (he listed many)…had reached the fulfillment of its age-old yearning-the return to a free and independent Zion...We danced-but we knew ahead of us lay the battlefield."

[220] Ibid pg. 182.

[221] Ibid pg. 155. Six thousand Jews die in the immediate aftermath of Independence (1% of the population).

[222] Ibid pg. 182.

[223] Ibid pg. 167.

[224] Wikipedia en.wikipedia.org/wiki/1949_Armistice_Agreements.

[225] Jerusalem Islamic Waqf… "best known for controlling and managing current Islamic edifices around and including the Al-Aqsa Mosque in the Old City of Jerusalem." Wikipedia 9/3/15.

The Balfour Declaration 1917

Foreign Office,
November 2nd, 1917.

Dear Lord Rothschild,

I have much pleasure in conveying to you, on behalf of His Majesty's Government, the following declaration of sympathy with Jewish Zionist aspirations which has been submitted to, and approved by, the Cabinet

"His Majesty's Government view with favour the establishment in Palestine of a national home for the Jewish people, and will use their best endeavours to facilitate the achievement of this object, it being clearly understood that nothing shall be done which may prejudice the civil and religious rights of existing non-Jewish communities in Palestine, or the rights and political status enjoyed by Jews in any other country"

I should be grateful if you would bring this declaration to the knowledge of the Zionist Federation.

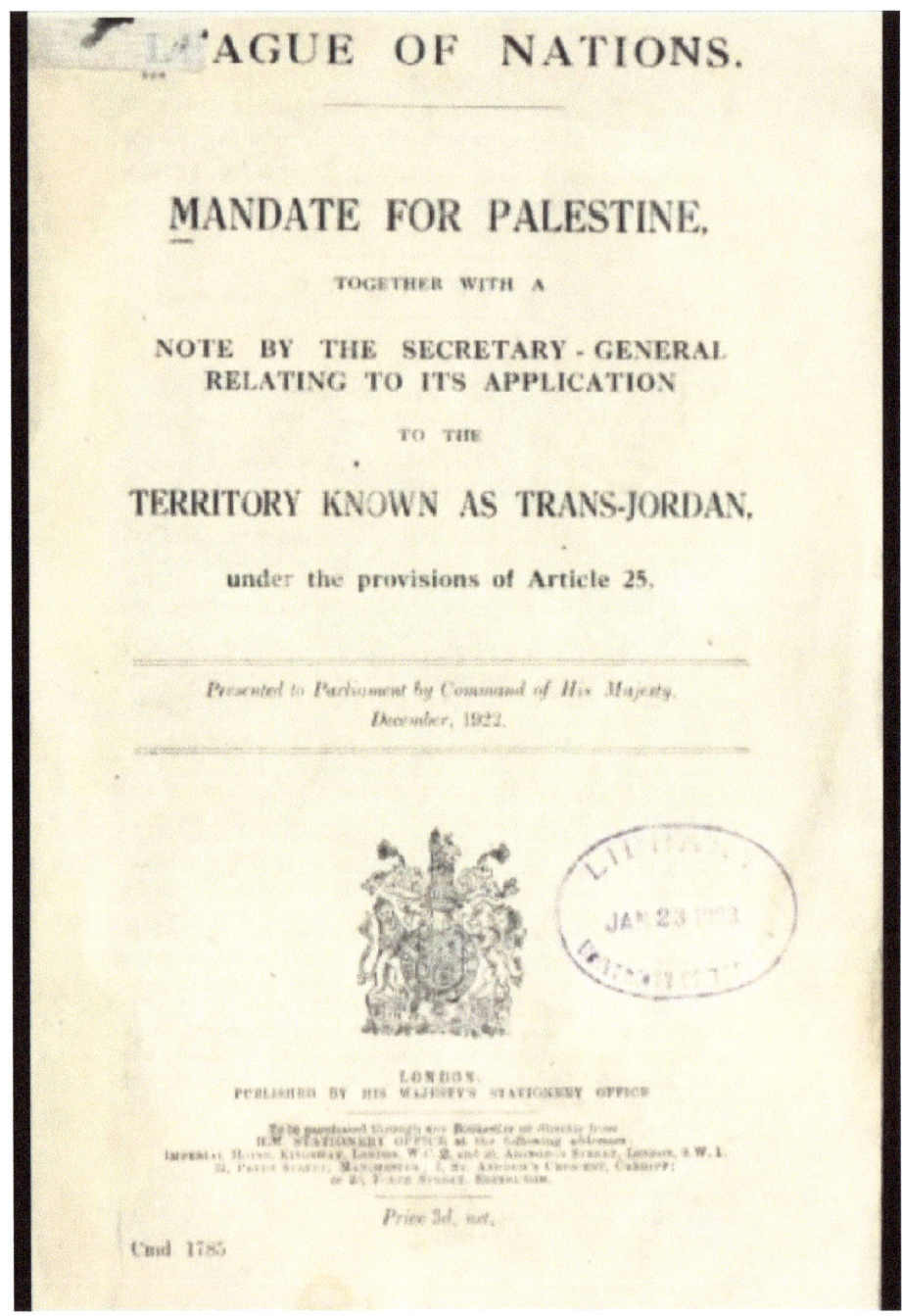

British Command Paper 1785, December 1922, containing the **Mandate for Palestine and the Transjordan** memorandum

Created 1920-2 From Wikipedia 9-16-15 online public Domain
Ratified 1923
Signatories League of Nations
Purpose Creation of the territories of Palestine and Transjordan

Creation of the State of Israel
May 14, 1948

"The Israeli Declaration of Independence (Hakhrazat HaAtzma'ut or Megilat HaAtzma'ut), formally the Declaration of the Establishment of the State of Israel, was proclaimed on 14 May 1948 (5 Iyar 5708) by David Ben-Gurion, the Executive Head of the World Zionist Organization and the chairman of the Jewish Agency for Palestine. It declared the establishment of a Jewish state in Eretz-Israel, to be known as the State of Israel, which would come into effect on termination of the British Mandate at midnight that day. The event is celebrated annually in Israel with a national holiday Yom Ha'atzmaut (lit. Independence Day) on 5 Iyar of every year according to the Hebrew calendar."

Immigration of Jewish People to Israel 1947-Part of the Aliyah.

David Ben Gurion signs Declaration of Independence May 14, 1948

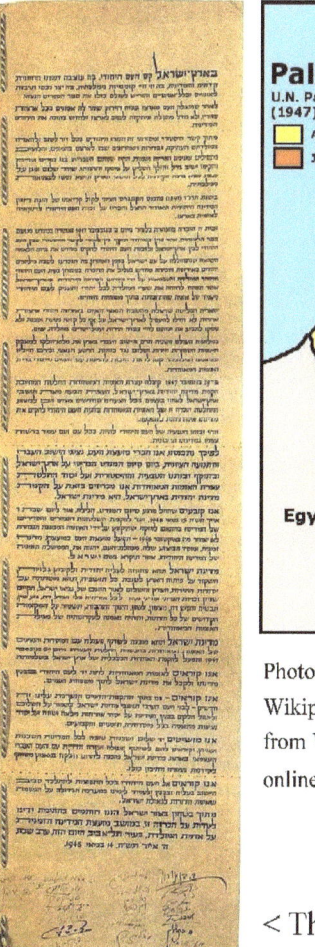

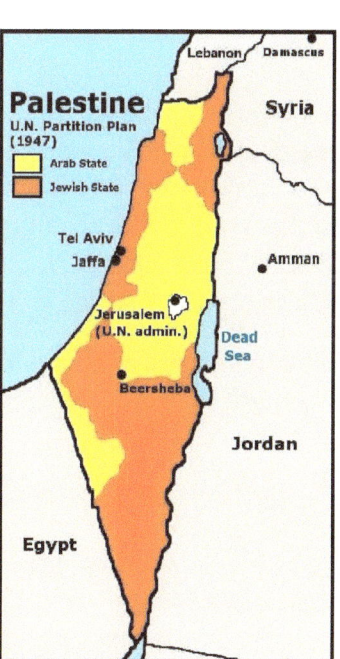

Photos public domain on Wikipedia 6-12-16. Comments from Wikipedia *History of Israel* online 6-14-16.

< The Israel Declaration of Independence

History of Israel from 1918-1948 (Coins in use in Palestine)

"Palestine was a part of the Turkish empire in 1917, when it was captured by British troops. It remained under British military administration until July 24, 1924, when it became a British Mandate under the League of Nations. The mandate was abolished at midnight, May 14, 1948, when Israel became an independent state."[226]

As such, coins were produced for Palestine written in Hebrew, Arabic, and English. These coins were produced from 1927 to 1947. They were designed and stamped by the Royal Mint. Coins were struck in "denominations of 1, 2, 5, 10, 20, 50, and 100 mils. The 1 and 2 mils were struck in bronze, whilst the 5, 10 and 20 mils were holed, cupro-nickel coins, except for during World War II, when they were also minted in bronze. The 50 and 100 mil coins were struck in .720 silver."[225] (These coins were recalled in the 1950's by the Israeli government.)[227]

1) Palestine Mandate 5 mil Coin dated 1927: Obv. "Around central hole, a wreath of olive leaves surrounded by 'Palestine' in English above, Hebrew to left, and Arabic to right; below, the date in English and Arabic numerals." Rev. "Around central hole, inscriptions '5 MILS' in English, Arabic, and Hebrew, the numeral 5 of the English phrase at top."[226]

2) Haganah Defense Token: This token was developed in 1936 as a way to tax the population of Palestine so as to support the Jewish Defense Forces. They were a militia set up to protect Jewish groups from Arabic uprisings against them. It was developed by a group of individuals, the "Kofer Hayeshuv (Redemption of the Country)". The token was worth ½ mil (1000 Mils=Palestine Pound), and stamped at the "Plitz factory in Holon."[228]

3) Palestine Mandate 2 Mil Coin dated 1942: Obv. "Palestine in Arabic, English, and Hebrew; date below in English and Arabic numerals." Rev. "In center, seven-leaved olive branch dividing numerals '2' on left in English, in Arabic on right; above, 'TWO MILS' in English, 'MILS' to left in Hebrew, to right in Arabic."[226]

---

[226] History of Modern Israel's Money from 1917 to 1967 by Sylvia Haffner, 1st ed. 1976, San Diego CA. p. 77, 118, 122, 123.
[227] Wikipedia http://en.wikipedia.org/wiki/Palestine_pound
[228] Haganah Defense Token p.122 in Haffner book.

History of Israel from 1918 to 1948

(Coins not to Relative Size)

CHAPTER 10   HISTORY OF THE JEWS 1947/48 - CURRENT

1947-1951
Once England allowed immigration into Israel, Jews migrated in mass numbers: 686,739 in those years even though England held a large number of them on Cyprus till 1949. They came from seventy different countries. Those from Iraq "lost everything"; 90,000 were airlifted. They went to Iran to catch planes. As well, large numbers of Arabs would leave Israel, upwards of 4 million, to the surrounding Arab countries.[229]

1952
Germany paid 3,450 million Marks ($865 million) to the Israeli government to assist German Jews now in Israel; very few were in Germany itself post WW2.[230]

1953
Holocaust Martyrs' and Heroes' Remembrance Authority was set up, 8/19/53, using a verse from Isaiah: "Even unto them will I give within My house and within My walls a monument and a memorial…everlasting memorial, which will never be cut off." The testimony of survivors of the holocaust were recorded, and of non-Jews that helped them.[231]

Hebrew University was opened, and Israeli Arab students were allowed to attend.

Violence between Arab terrorists and counter-attacks by Israel would continue.

Archaeology became an important field for the Jewish government. "The new state's search for its roots made every major archaeological discovery a matter of national importance." The Dead Sea Scrolls, some found initially by an Arab sheep herder, would be highly sought after. Sukenik would buy some in 1952. Yadin would travel to the US to obtain others ($250,000 for the scroll of Isaiah and others) in 1953-54.[232]

---

[229] Israel by Martin Gilbert pg. 256-57.
[230] Ibid pg. 283.
[231] Ibid pg. 288-89.
[232] Ibid pg. 295.

1947 Partition Map of Israel: Jews and Arabs Re-establishment of the Land of Israel

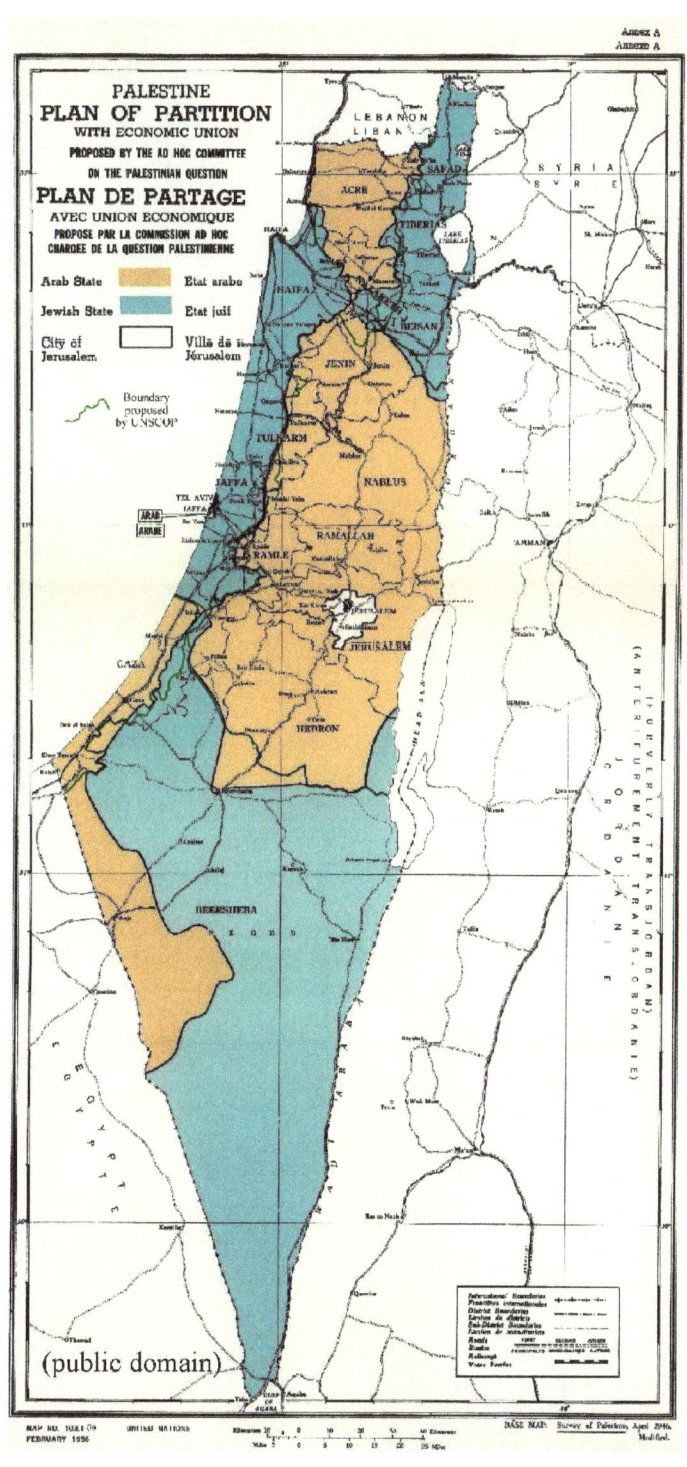

1955
Israel started up its first nuclear reactor.[233]

12/1955-10/1956 War Syria attacked northern Israel in the Sea of Galilee area in 12/55 on Hanukah. Egypt blocked the Gulf of Aquiba. Israel struck back with Moshe Dayan as its military leader in 10/56. A ceasefire was obtained on 11/7/56.

1950's-1960's
Continued skirmishes occurred on borders and the Jordan River water usage rights were contested. Egypt built up Russian armament.[234] Israel's neighbors, Lebanon, Syria, Jordan, and Egypt, still considered themselves to be in a state of war with it, and "fedayeen across the border from Gaza were almost continuous."[235]

1960
Adolf Eichmann, administrator of the Nazi Holocaust, was caught in Argentina and hung in 1962.[236]

1963
Yadin excavated at Masada. Water system was developed to take water from the Jordan River to the Negev. This project was opposed by the Arab countries.[237]

1966
France stopped supplying arms to Israel, but US agreed to. President Nassar of Egypt threatened war if UN did not remove troops from the Sinai.[238]

1967 The Six Day War
Events leading to the war included the closing of the Straits of Tehran to Israeli shipping. Israeli ambassador met a favorable response from US President Johnson regarding a group of nations re-opening the route. Nassar commented, "The battle will be a general one"… "and our basic objective will be to destroy Israel."[239]

Arab supplies: 100,000 men and 900 tanks on Egyptian front but could send another 140,000 men and 300 tanks; 75,000 men and 400 tanks on the Golan Heights, 32,000 men and 300 tanks on the Jordan side, and 150 tanks from Iraq, and 700 combat aircraft from all the countries.

Israeli supplies: 240,000 men (with civilian reserves), 800 tanks, and 300 aircraft.[240]

---

[233] Ibid pg. 301.
[234] History of Israel online Wikipedia 9-15-15.
[235] Israel by Martin Gilbert pg. 310.
[236] Ibid
[237] Ibid.
[238] Ibid.
[239] Israel by Martin Gilbert pg. 373.
[240] Ibid pg. 381.

Israel peremptorily struck the air forces of Egypt, Jordan and Syria and destroyed many on the ground in June. The Arab combined ground forces were defeated in November and a ceasefire was called. Israel gained many areas which would be given back later.[241]

Jews from Russia were hindered from immigrating to Israel by Russian authorities.[242]

1968
Palestinian camps in Jordan were attacked by Israel for planting land mines in Israel.[243]

US supplied arms to Israel, while France still had an embargo and Russia continued to supply Arab states with military aid. "The Eshkol-Johnson agreement marked the beginning of an arms race which transformed the United States into Israel's major arms supplier, and pitted the United States against the Soviet Union through their respective client States in the Middle East."[244]

1969-1974
Golda Meir gave years of service to Israel. A Russian born Jew, she had been Minister of Labor since 1949. She became Prime Minister in 1969. Her first statements included, "We are prepared to discuss peace with our neighbors, all day and on all matters." Part of Nassar's response was, "What was lost in war must be restored by war." What would follow was a "War of Attrition".[245] Meir offered to go to Egypt to develop a compromise plan with Nassar but it was rebuffed by him and derided by other Arab States.[246]

1970
Abba Eban wrote in the London Times that Arab States had a population of 100 million, four million square miles of land, "vast mineral wealth and opportunities of creative growth…the Arab nation has come off better than most. On the other side of the conflict is the small State of Israel. Arab nationhood and sovereignty are thus assured beyond doubt or challenge, and Israel is the only nation which stands or falls in history by the way in which the conflict is resolved. Thus Israel's security is the overriding moral imperative in this dispute." He then would then argue that the "central issue" for the Arab States should not be Palestinian self-determination but "the duty of peace with Israel…"[247]

Yassar Arafat commented during the same time period, "The Palestinian revolution's basic concern is the uprooting of the Zionist entity from our land and liberating it."[248]

The PLO was driven out of Jordan by King Hussein (they went to Lebanon).[249]

---

[241] Wikipedia History of Israel online 9-15-15.
[242] Ibid.
[243] Ibid.
[244] Israel by Martin Gilbert pg. 407.
[245] Facts About Israel: History www.mfa.gov.il?MFA/About Israel/History. online9-15-15. It would be called "Egypt's War of Attrition Against Israel" from 1968-70.
[246] Ibid pg. 410.
[247] Ibid pg. 412.
[248] Ibid pg. 418.
[249] History of Israel Wikipedia.

1972
Munich Olympics: Eleven Jewish athletes were killed. Israel struck the PLO headquarters in Lebanon. Anwar Sedat expelled Soviet advisors from Egypt.[250]

1973 Yom Kippur War (The October War)[251]
Libya had sent "terrorist squads" into both Israel and Jordan.

Austria stopped helping to assist Jews from Russia, now able to leave, from staying in Austria till they could get to Israel. Arab countries encouraged other European nations to do the same, as well as a demand that Israel return lands captured during the Six Day War.

Syria placed "hundreds" of tanks along the demarcation line. Syria had 1200 and Israel 170 there.

Syria and Egypt attacked Israel on Israel's holy day, the "Day of Atonement". Yitzhak Rabin recalled, "One didn't have to be a former Chief of Staff to realize that the IDF was on alert footing, but even so I never expected war." Initially, when the sirens alarmed they were turned off because it was a holy day, but were then re-assumed. Because of intelligence information regarding an attack on the holy day Golda Meir agreed to a partial mobilization of men the day before.

Egypt crossed the Suez Canal with tanks the first day "with fighting on land and in the air." 240 aircraft and 2000 artillery guns attacked. Within one minute 10,000 shells were fired and the shelling continued 43 minutes. Eight thousand Egyptian soldiers would cross the canal.

Syria attacked on the Golan Heights with 1400 tanks. Syrian planes attacked at the same time as the Egyptian ones in their areas.

Gilbert commented regarding the 1973 War, "For the Israeli troops there was as no swift advance and no clear cut sweep to victory as there had been in 1956 and 1967. Unlike those two wars, the October battle was one in which, at many moments, the tide could have turned against the Israeli forces." He was referring to the Suez Canal but the whole contest was touch and go.[252] Toward the end of the War Israel would control the ground and air in that area.

Idi Amin of Uganda encouraged Arab troops not to cease hostilities.[253]

On October 22, 1973 a ceasefire was agreed upon. UN observers were sent to plant ceasefire flags. Syrian casualties in the Golan 3,500 and Israeli 722; Arab tanks 1,500 incapacitated (867 recovered), Israeli tanks 350 (250 recovered); on both fronts Israel lost 2,522 combatants, the losses among the Arab nations were not mentioned.[254] Gilbert comments about 3 consequences of the war for Israel: 1) Its crucial need of support from the United States, 2) the Third World's break off of diplomatic relations post war increased Israel's isolation as the Communist Bloc had broken off relations after the 1967 War; and 3) while Israel had won, the fact that Egypt had initially broken through the Suez Canal area gave them a sense of "self-assertion."[255]

---
[250] Ibid
[251] Israel Martin Gilbert pg. 426-461. See these pages for all quotes regarding the 1973 Yom Kippur War.
[252] Israel Martin Gilbert pg. 453.
[253] Ibid 458.
[254] Ibid pg. 460.
[255] Ibid pg. 460.

1974-77
Yitzhak Rabin was elected as Prime Minister after Golda Meir resigned due to criticism of her handling of the Yom Kippur War.

1974
Egypt came to a cessation of hostilities, but the Golan Heights continued to be contested by Syria. Terrorism within Israel continued; Palestinians attacked a school in Ma'alot and killed 22 children, and a family in Northern Israel.[256]

1975
Egypt and Israel, with Henry Kissinger presiding, signed agreements over the Sinai. As well, the US agreed to not "treat", that is negotiate, with the PLO as a terrorist organization. "For Rabin, this agreement was fashioned on his 'peace doctrine' of five phases: Disengagement, Defusion, Trust, Negotiations, Peace (the Oslo Agreement was later to follow the same model)."[257]

1976
An Air France plane was hijacked by the PLO and taken to Uganda (Idi Amin was still president). Israel commandos rescued the Jews (97) and non-Jews. One Jew was lost: Yoni Netanyahu (the brother of the future Prime Minister Benjamin Netanyahu). Rabin commented, "We do not bask in the glory of such victories. We do remember, in sorrow and pride, the men who gave their lives, at Entebbe and elsewhere in the defense of Israel, that this nation should live in peace and dignity in its land."[258]

1977- 83
Menachem Begin was elected Prime Minister. He had been born in Ashkenazi, Poland and survived WW2. He introduced Biblical terms for the West Bank: Samaria and Judea. He fully supported West Bank settlement by Jewish groups, which US President Jimmy Carter opposed.[259]

1977
Sadat traveled to Jerusalem to meet with Begin, and addressed the Kennesset. He pledged, "Tell your sons that the past war was the last of wars and the end of sorrows." Many in Israeli society opposed the visit as well as in Arab circles.[260]

---

[256] Ibid pg. 466. Even with these activities an Arab summit on 10/25/74 would recognize the PLO (Palestinian Liberation Organization) as the "sole representative of the Palestinian people." Article 22 of its National Covenant described Zionism as "a racist and fanatical movement in its formation; aggressive, expansionist and colonist in its aims, and Fascist and Nazi in its means." See pg. 467.

[257] Ibid pg. 468.

[258] Ibid pg. 473.

[259] Ibid pg. 480-81. He argued for an East Bank home for the Palestinians in Jordan. He considered the PLO on the West Bank to be a "mortal danger" to Israel. He would agree to "substantial withdrawals" from the Sinai; Israel would stay on the Golan Heights, but was willing to "accommodate" the US regarding the new settlements but hard for him to restrict the influx of settlers into existing settlements.

[260] Ibid pg. 489. He would be assassinated on 10/6/81 by the Egyptian Islamic Jihad with a *fatwa* approval from Omar Adel-Raham (later involved in the World Trade Center bombing of 1993). Assassination of Anwar Sadat- Wikipedia . Gilbert pg. 499 commented, "Among his alleged 'crimes' was having made peace with Israel."

1978

Camp David Accord (9/17/78): "called for the 'normalization' of relations between Israel and Egypt, to be followed by Jordan, Syria and Lebanon. At the timing of the signing, none of these three countries showed the slightest interest in pursuing such a call."[261] Only Sadat, Begin, and Carter met. Many within Israel did not agree with Begin giving up the settlements in parts of the Sinai and at the entrance to the Gulf of Akaba.[262]

1979

The Peace Treaty between Israel and Egypt was signed on March 20th by the Knesset. Both Begin and Sadat received the Nobel Peace Prize on December 10, 1979 for their involvement.[263]

Forty thousand Iraqi Jews were allowed to immigrate to Israel.[264]

1981

Israeli Air Force destroyed the Iraqi nuclear reactor before it became operational.[265]

1982

Israel completed withdrawal from the Sinai.[266]
Lebanon War: purpose to drive the PLO out of Lebanon. It lasted from June 1982 to August 1982. It was called "Operation Peace for Galilee by Israel." [267]

1985

Gilbert comments on the diversity of Jewish society in 1985: "The nature of Israel was an unusual, perhaps a unique mixture of peoples and customs. The unifying factor was their Jewishness, but many strands of Judaism and Jewishness that evolved in the Diaspora since the destruction of the Second Temple by the Romans 2,000 years earlier made for complex and often conflicting lifestyles and attitudes. Unlike any other State, a majority of Israel's inhabitants were immigrants, and they came from very different linguistic, social and cultural backgrounds. In 1985 Israel's Jewish population consisted of only 18.5 per cent native born Israelis."[268]

1987

The Intifada was started.[269]

---

[261] Ibid 492.
[262] Ibid 494,
[263] Ibid pg. 495.
[264] History of Israel-Wikipedia.
[265] Facts About Israel:History.
[266] Ibid.
[267] Ibid.
[268] Israel by Martin Gilbert pg. 519. Also Russians 21.3 %, Africa 22%, Europe and America 38.2 %.
[269] Ibid Chapter titled Intifada. A general rebellion against Israeli authority in Arabic villages in Israel and the West Bank. Many still lived in refuge camps. It lasted almost 5 years. Pg. 526.

1988

Hamas published its covenant. The PLO was not the sole representative of the Palestinian, and no permanent compromise with Israel was allowed.[270]

1989

Initiation of "mass migration of Jews from the former Soviet Union" began.[271] Within 2 two years 330,000 Jews immigrated from Russia and its associated states.[272]

In May 1989 Israeli soldiers were reprimanded for desecrating a Koran. In July thirty ultra-Orthodox Jews killed a thirteen year old girl near Nablis. Their leader was advised to review Haim Cohn's *Human Rights in the Bible and the Talmud* by the judge in the case.[273] The Intifada continued as well. Hebrew Scholar Menachem Stern was stabbed to death by two Arab youth in a West Jerusalem park in order to qualify for "membership of Yasser Arafat's Fatah."[274]

1990

Operation Solomon conducted an airlift of 4,137 Jews from Ethopia. About the same number had arrived over the last five years.[275]

1991

Israel was attacked by scud missiles from Iraq during the Gulf War.[276] Saddam Hussein connected any withdrawal from Kuwait with Israel returning "occupied territories". Israel was kept out of the Allied coalition so that Saudi Arabia would remain in it. England was given the task to seek out and destroy any scud missile sites that targeted Israel.[277]

1993

Oslo Accords (9/13/1993) were signed by Yasser Arafat and Yitzhak Rabin with US President Bill Clinton present: "Its main concern was on Israeli withdrawal from the territories of Judea, Samaria and the Gaza Strip, in order to allow the establishment of a Palestinian Authority for self-government for an interim period until permanent arrangements would be established."[278]

1994

Palestinian self-government as set up in the Gaza Strip and Jericho areas. Diplomatic relations with the Catholic Church were set up. Morocco and Tunisia offices were set up in Israel.[279]

---

[270] Ibid pg. 530.
[271] Facts About Israel:History.
[272] Israel Martin Gilbert pg. 537.
[273] Ibid pg. 539.
[274] Ibid pg. 541.
[275] Ibid pg. 537.
[276] Ibid.
[277] Ibid 546-7. Scuds were a particular problem as they could not be stopped. The transit time was 5-7 minutes. "Forty scuds fell on Tel Aviv, Ramat Gan and Haifa during the course of the war. Four thousand apartments were totally destroyed." Only one civilian was killed, and several hundred wounded. The US and the Netherlands would send Patriot missiles to defend Israel. The effectiveness was controversial, as well as the US involvement in Israel.
[278] www.Knesset.gov.il/lexicon/eng/oslo_eng.htm
[279] Facts About Israel: History.

1995
Yitzhak Rabin was assassinated. He was killed after a rally in which he had stated, "I was a military man for twenty-seven years. I fought as long as there was no chance for peace. I believe that there is now a chance for peace, a great chance."[280]

1996
Operation Grapes of Wrath took place: a retaliation for Hezbollah attacks on Northern Israel.[281] Binyamin Netanyahu was elected Prime Minister.

1997
Hebron Protocol was signed between Israel and the PLO.

1998
Wye River Memorandum was signed between Israel and the PLO.

2000
Israel withdrew from the Security Zone in southern Lebanon. Second intifada occurred.

2001- 2010[282]
Continued warfare with the Gaza Strip based terrorists occurred.

2001
Tenet Ceasefire Plan was proposed between Israel and the PLO.

2002
Operation Defensive Shield was launched by Israel second to Palestinian terrorists attacks. An Anti-terrorist Fence was set up to hinder terrorists from the Gaza Strip.

2006
Second Lebanon War happened against Hezbollah terrorists camps there.

2007
Continued hostilities from the Gaza Strip occurred towards Israel, as Hamas took over the area in 2007. There was destruction of a Nuclear Power Plant in Syria, having been set up there by North Korea.[283] This occurred during Operation Orchard.[284]

---

[280] *Israel* Martin Gilbert pg. 587. His murderer was a Jew Yigal Amir who felt Rabin had betrayed Jewish beliefs. Pg. 588-9. One million Jews would pass his coffin on 11/4/95. King Hussein, Jordan, President Mubarak Egypt, Prime Minister of Morocco, representative of Qatar and Oman, and members of eighty other countries came to his memorial.
[281] Facts About Israel: History.
[282] Ibid.
[283] You Tube Video by www.alternativehistory.com in 2007, and www.haaretz.com/news/diplomacy-defense/north-korea-supplying-syria-iran-with-prohibited-nuclear-technology-report-says-1.398295 in 2011.
[284] This action occurred on Sept. 6th 2007. It was confirmed to be a nuclear facility in 2011. Wikipedia "Operation Orchard."

2008
Operation Cast Lead was launched against the Gaza Strip for 10,000 rockets released from there.

2010
Israeli air strike killed 4 Islamic Jihad operatives.[285, 286] Terrorists continued Kassam rocket fire into Israeli communities. Israel joined the Organization for Economic Co-operation and Development. Israel continued negotiations with the Palestinians hosted by the US.

2011
Israeli navy intercepted a ship "Victoria" with 50 tons of weapons headed for Gaza Strip.[287,288] Israel developed the Iron Dome anti-missile system that successfully shot down rockets fired by Hamas from the Gaza Strip. John Demjanjuk was found guilty as an accessory to the murders of Jewish people in Nazi Germany in WW2. Netanyahu addressed the UN after Mahmoud Abbas requested UN recognize the State of Palestine. Continued firing of rockets from Gaza into Israel occurred.

2012
Clay shard was found in Jerusalem with inscription name of Bethlehem.

2014-2015
Destruction of a Syrian chemical weapons factory was successfully carried out. Israel sent relief aid to Philippine victims of a typhoon, and to Nepal after a large earthquake. Israel sent a fleet of Cobra helicopters to Jordan to assist in monitoring the border. A Mikveh, ritual bathhouse, was uncovered in Jerusalem.

On 9/13/15 a pipe bomb was found at the Mughraki Gate just before Jews celebrate Rosh Hashanah. It is the only gate to the Temple Mount for non-Arabs. On 9/14/15 Muslims threw rocks at non-Muslims trying to enter the Temple Mount to pray. Israelis opened the gate for parishioners to gain access to the Mount so as to pray. On 9/15/15 Arab leaders from various countries said action is a "declaration of war".[289]

Population of Israel in 2015: total 8,412,000; 74.9 % Jewish (6,300,000) and 20.7% Arab (1,746,000); 4.7 % others (366,000- Christian, Baha'i etc.). Growth rate 1.9% with Jewish growth 1.75 and Arabic 2.2%. Total Jewish population in the world: 14,200,000 with 43% living in Israel.[290] Israel is surrounded by Arab/Islamic nations who have 90-100% Muslim population. See figure next page as well as Zechariah 12:1-9.

2016
Prime Minister Netanyahu stated, "We live in an era…(where there's) ongoing multinational hostility to Israel. You see it at the UN;…UN Human Rights Council…the ICC…the EU." He then went on to say that there are many independent countries coming to Israel because of their concerns regarding militant Islam and looking for Israel's help.[291]

---

[285] www.jewishvirtuallibrary.org/source/History/time 2010s.
[286] Ibid.
[287] Ibid.
[288] Ibid.
[289] US Strikes Syrian Chemical Weapons Stockpile on 8/18/2014. Assad continued to use chlorine gas against Syrian non-Islamic peoples. www.JewishVirtualLibrary.com
[290] www.JewishVirtualLibrary.com
[291] http://www.jewishvirtuallibrary.org/jsources/US-Israel/netan21416.html

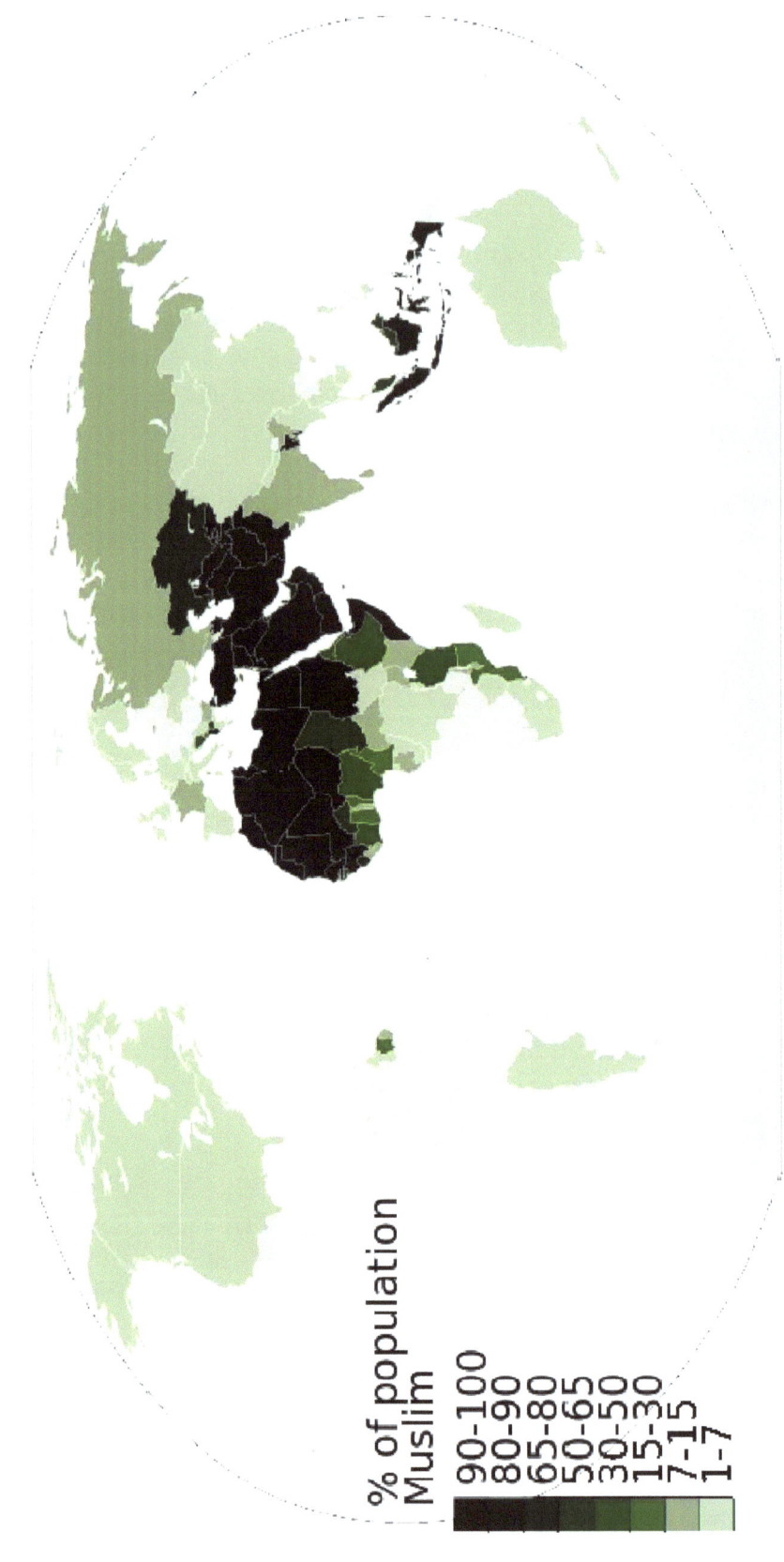

Middle East Countries
(CIA map public domain 6-16-16)

CHAPTER 11   JEWISH POPULATION AND TIMELINE OF THEIR HISTORY

Jewish World Population in Various Time Periods[292]

1000 BC: About 5,000,000 (Time of David the King)[293]

1200 AD: 2,000,000[294]

1880: 7,800,000

1922: 14,400,000

1939: 16,728,000

1945: 11,000,000[295]

1970: 12,585,000

2014: 13,900,000

Percent of Total Population (Within a Country) in Various Regions now:

Americas: United States 1.8%, Canada 1.09%, Guatemala (other South American countries) <0.01%; Total population 957,830,000; Jewish 6,468,800; % Jewish 0.67%

Asia: Israel 74%, Yemen (and other Mid-East nations) <0.01%; Total population 4,224,800,000; Jewish 6,142,000; % Jewish 0.14%

Oceania: Australia 0.49%, New Zealand 0.17%; Total Population 138,000,000; Jewish 120,100; % Jewish 0.32%

Africa: Ethiopia (and other African Nations) <0.01%; Total population 1,100,000,000; Jewish 74,700; % Jewish 0.01%

Europe: Romania 0.04%, U.K 0.45%, Poland 0.01%, Russia 0.13%; Total population 816,890,000; Jewish 1,407,200; % Jewish 0.17%

---

[292] https://www.jewishvirtuallibrary.org/jsource/Judaism/jewpop.html
[293] "The Census of David is said to have recorded 1,300,000 males over twenty years of age, which would imply a population of over 5,000,000. The number of exiles who returned from Babylon is given at 42,360. Tacitus declares that Jerusalem at its fall contained 600,000 persons; Josephus, that there were as many as 1,100.000 slain in the destruction of Jerusalem in AD 70, along with 97,000 who were sold as slaves. However, Josephus also qualifies this count, noting that Jerusalem was besieged during the Passover. The majority of the 1,197,000 would not have been residents of the city, but rather visiting for the festival…By the early 13th century, the world Jewish population had fallen to 2 million from a peak at 8 million during the 1st century, with only 250,000 living in Christian lands. Many factors had devastated the Jewish population, including the Bar Kochba Revolt and the First Crusade." Wikipedia "Historical Jewish Populations Comparisons" online 11-7-2015.
[294] Ibid.
[295] This represents a loss of nearly six million Jewish people in the German Gas Chambers during WW2.

Timeline of Mankind
(Approximately)

Adam	4000 BC			
			Noah's Flood	
	3000 BC		2300*	
		Jews in Land	Egypt Jews out of Land	Joshua Jews in the Land
Abra-ham	2000 BC			
	King David Jews in the Land 1000	Babylon Jews out of Land	Persia----Greek-----Rome Jews in the Land	
	Rome Jews in the Land 0 BC/AD	Bysantine Jews out of the Land 135 AD	Islam	
Jesus Christ	Crusades 1000	Nations of the Earth Jews out of the Land	Jews in the Land 1948	
	Jews in the Land 2000 AD	(Soon to come Millennial Reign of Christ In the Land)		

* **Genesis 11:10** tells us that Shem was 100 years old, 2 years after the Flood had finished. When was Noah's Flood? 1,981 years to AD 1 plus 967 years to the founding of Solomon's Temple plus 480 years to the end of the Exodus plus 430 years to the promise to Abraham plus 75 years to Abraham's birth plus 350 years to Shem's 100th birthday plus 2 years to the Flood. The Biblical data places the Flood at 2304 BC ± 11 years. http://creation.com/the-date-of-noahs-flood

CHAPTER 12   MODERN ISRAELI COINAGE AND MEDALS

(Representative but not entire series, many with ancient motifs, not comparative in size)

1) Fifty Prutot. 1949-1980

Obv. Grape leaf on vine. Inscription in Hebrew "Israel" above and in Arabic below. Rev. Olive branches along edge with inscription in Hebrew "50 Pruta-5709" not shown. Cupronickel 23.5 mm, wt 5.6 gm. From HMIM, p-15, pg. 23. Right : Obv. of Jewish War coin with grape leaf on vine from 70 AD.

2) One Hundred Prutot. 1949-1980. (This coin is from 1949)

Obv. Seven branched palm tree with two clusters of dates. Inscription "Israel" in Hebrew above and Arabic below. Rev. Wreath of olive branches. Inscription "100 Pruta-5709" in Hebrew. Cupronickel, 28.5 mm, 11.3 gm. From HMIM, p-20, pg. 24. Right: Obv. of Bar Kochba War with similar seven branched palm tree and two clusters of dates from 134/5 AD.

3) One Pruta. 1949-1980.

Left: Obv. Ancient anchor. Inscription "Israel" in Hebrew above and Arabic below. Has a "pearl". Rev. Olive branches. Inscription "1 Pruta-5709" in Hebrew. Aluminum, 21 mm, wt. 1.3 gm. (Not shown) Middle: Obv. Herod the Great coin with anchor symbolic of the Selucid Kingdom from 4 BC. Right: Obv. Hyracanus 1 coin with anchor from 132 BC. HMIM p-3, pg. 18.

4) One Agora. 1960-1980.

Obv. Stalks of barley with ten ears on the left and eight on the other two stalks. Inscription in Hebrew "Israel" at the base and in Arabic along the left side. Rev. Numeral One "Agora" at base but above the date "1960" in Hebrew. Right: Stocks of barley from Herod Agrippa 1 coin in 42 AD. HMIM a-102, pg. 30.

5) New Sheqalim. Current exchange.

Left: Obv. Two cornucopia with barley stalks and date clusters. Center Pomegranate. Small symbol top center emblem of Israel (with menorah). Small pearls around sides. Rev. Numeral two centered. Inscription "Israel" in Arabic left upper English Hebrew right upper. Below numeral in Hebrew and English Arabic "New Sheqalim." Image online Wikipedia 7-2015 public domain. Right: Maccabean coin with cornucopia date 132 BC.

Modern Israeli Coinage 1948-Current

(Representative but not entire series. Many with ancient motifs)

(not representative of size)

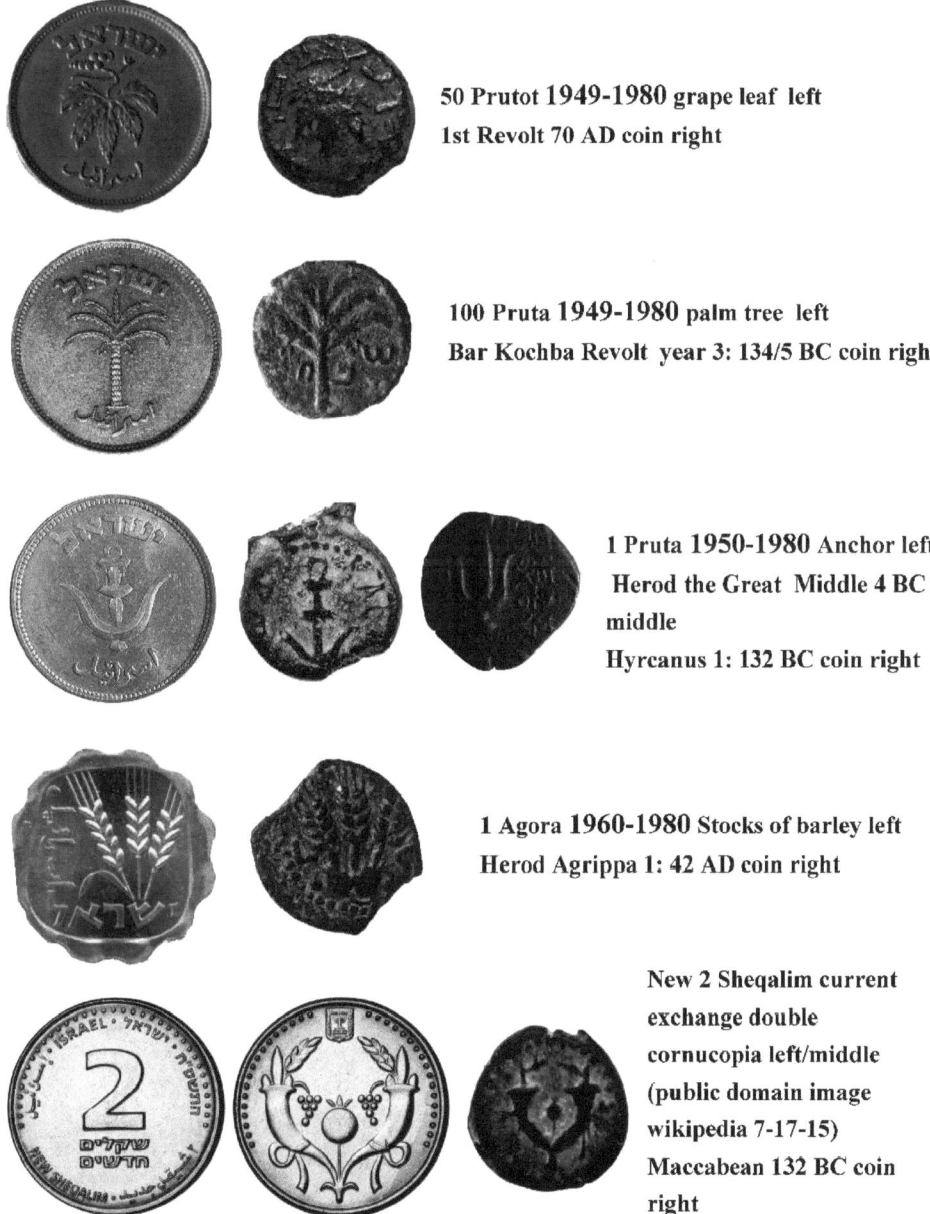

50 Prutot 1949-1980 grape leaf left
1st Revolt 70 AD coin right

100 Pruta 1949-1980 palm tree left
Bar Kochba Revolt year 3: 134/5 BC coin right

1 Pruta 1950-1980 Anchor left
Herod the Great Middle 4 BC in middle
Hyrcanus 1: 132 BC coin right

1 Agora 1960-1980 Stocks of barley left
Herod Agrippa 1: 42 AD coin right

New 2 Sheqalim current exchange double cornucopia left/middle (public domain image wikipedia 7-17-15)
Maccabean 132 BC coin right

Medals of Israel 1960's

1) Judea Capta Israel Liberation Medal. 1962 Obv. Center small replica of Roman Judea Capta coin. Inscription in Hebrew above and English below "Judea Capta 70 AD". Rev. Large seven branched palm tree, symbolic of Judea with woman raising a child in the air and man planting sapling. Inscription Hebrew above "Israel Liberated 5718" and English "Israel Liberated 1948". Edge inscription in Hebrew and English "state of Israel". HMIM m-21, pg. 161. Mint 25, 000; 59 mm, wt 118 gm.

2) Israeli Armed Forces Remembrance Day Medal. 1963 Given to families of those who had fallen in battle. Obv. Divided by palm leaves with an emblem of a woman raising her child into the air and a man planting a sapling right upper and on left "To the memory of those who fell for its independence" and "Ministry of Defense." On rim inscription, "Israel Liberated". Rev. A chain divides the coin and a small replica of a Roman Judea Capta coin in the upper right with Roman soldier looking over weeping Jew. Inscription on left in Hebrew "Remembrance Day for the fallen of the Israel Defence Army 5723." Along right edge "Judea Capta 3830". HMIM 60 mm, 120 gm, bronze. Pg. 166.

3) First Blockade Runners Medal. 1964 Obv. Mediterranean and Black Seas with routes of blockade runners going to Israel. Inscription in Hebrew above and English below "30th Anniversary of the first immigrant runners." Rev. Barbed wire fence on Palestine Coast and a runner bursting through. Dead Sea and Jordan River at base and inscription below, "Deut: 1, 41" in Hebrew and English. HMIM M-31, 59 mm, 110 gm. Bronze, pg. 172.

4) Jerusalem Medal. 1966 Obv. Stylized version of Jerusalem on a mountain with clouds above and within a Hebrew inscription "mountains Round about Jerusalem" with English below. Rev. Replica of Bar Kochba coin with Temple frontise and inscription around edge "Bar Kochba coin of Jerusalem" in Hebrew and English. HMIM # m-46, 45 mm, bronze, pg 188.

5) Israel Victory Coin. 1967 Obv. Sword with olive leaf and inscription around edge "Israel" in Hebrew English, and Arabic. 10 Lirot in Hebrew. Rev. Wailing Wall with inscription 1967 in English and Hebrew. Is. Gov. Medal Corp. c/142, 37 mm, wt 26 gm, silver. "28th day of year 5727" in Hebrew and "1967" in English.

Medals of Israel
(A Sampling)

1962 Medal of Liberation

1963 Israel Armed Forces Remembrance Day Medal

1964 First Immigrant Blockade Runners Medal

1966 Jerusalem Medal

1967 Israel's Anniversary Medal

Medals of Israel 1959, 1978, 1989, and 2000

1) Israel 50th Anniversary Tel Aviv. 1959 Obv. Waves of Mediterranean Sea lap against barren sand hills/dunes-reflecting the humble beginnings of Tel Aviv. Inscription, "Though thy beginning was small, yet thy latter end will greatly increase Job VIII:VII." Rev. Schematic of Tel Aviv about 1959 as a "large and prosperous city."[296] Bronze, 59 mm, 120 gm.

2) Pilgrimage to the Holy Land. 1978 Obv. Ancient 16th C map of Heinrich Bintung with Jerusalem at the center of three continents. Inscription "Holy Land" in Hebrew and "Terra Sancta" in Latin.[297] Rev. Inscription "They all gather and come to you Isaiah 60:4. Edge State emblem and inscription "State of Israel" in Hebrew and English, and serial number. Bronze, 59 mm, 98 gm.

3) Jews Fighting Against the Nazis. 1989 Obv. Flagpole with Star of David flying over a broken swastika and torn German Nazi flag. Inscription "Victory Over The Nazis" in Hebrew and English. Rev. Heads of Jewish soldiers representing those serving in Eretz Israel, USA, Great Britain, and the USSR. Inscription "Jewish Fighters Against Nazis 1939-1989" in Hebrew and English. Edge inscription "State of Israel" in Hebrew and English. Bronze, 70 mm, wt 120-140 gm.

4) The Great Year 2000 Jubilee/Holy Land/Garden Tomb. 2000 Obv. Image of the Garden Tomb in Jerusalem. Inscription "The Great Jubilee The Holy Land in English." Rev. Image of 2 fish and loaves of bread mosaic from ancient synagogue. Inscription "The Great 2000 Jubilee The Holy Land in English." Medal produced for visitors especially during the Pope's visit to the Holy Land. Bronze, 70 mm, 140 gm.

---

[296] See http://sheqel.info/5-1.htm
[297] Http://Israelmint.com.

Israel Medals 1959, 1978, 1989, and 2000

CHAPTER 13   JEWS IN THE LAND IN THE LAST DAYS

Psalm 147: "Praise the LORD! For it is good to sing praises to our God; for it is pleasant *and* praise is becoming. ²The LORD builds up Jerusalem; He gathers the outcasts of Israel. ³He heals the brokenhearted and binds up their wounds. ⁴He counts the number of the stars; He gives names to all of them. ⁵Great is our Lord and abundant in strength; His understanding is infinite."

Isaiah 11: ¹¹"Then it will happen on that day that the Lord will again recover the second time with His hand the remnant of His people, who will remain, from Assyria, Egypt, Pathros, Cush, Elam, Shinar, Hamath, and from the islands of the sea. ¹²And He will lift up a standard for the nations and assemble the banished ones of Israel, and will gather the dispersed of Judah from the four corners of the earth. … ¹⁶And there will be a highway from Assyria for the remnant of His people who will be left, just as there was for Israel in the day that they came up out of the land of Egypt."

(He prophesied the return from Babylon 200 years prior to the event. Yet, these scriptures also refer to a future time as seen in the verses below.)

Isaiah 11: "⁴But with righteousness He will judge the poor, and decide with fairness for the afflicted of the earth; and He will strike the earth with the rod of His mouth, and with the breath of His lips He will slay the wicked. ⁵Also righteousness will be the belt about His loins, and faithfulness the belt about His waist. ⁶And the wolf will dwell with the lamb, and the leopard will lie down with the young goat, and the calf and the young lion and the fatling together; and a little boy will lead them. ⁷Also the cow and the bear will graze, their young will lie down together, and the lion will eat straw like the ox. ⁸The nursing child will play by the hole of the cobra, and the weaned child will put his hand on the viper's den. ⁹They will not hurt or destroy in all My holy mountain, for the earth will be full of the knowledge of the LORD As the waters cover the sea. ¹⁰Then in that day the nations will resort to the root of Jesse, Who will stand as a signal for the peoples; and His resting place will be glorious."

Even though Israel is surrounded by nations that are predominantly Islamic, God will preserve the Jewish people. They have again been established in the Land, and many people groups, including Arabic peoples, will come to worship the Lord in Jerusalem (Isaiah 2:3).

CHAPTER 14   CONCLUSIONS

Coinage has played an important part in the history of mankind. It has reflected the economic systems that people have been bound to, the political aspiration and even the indoctrination of the leaders that ruled them, and the gods to whom they bowed their knees. It is also a tremendous archaeological tool; coins can be used to specifically date archaeological sites and correlate events surrounding those sites.

The scriptures have an interesting comment to make about coins in that Jesus said the love of money is a root of evil and not the money itself. Our present society is driven by a bottom dollar mentality which often over rides common sense, compassion, and morals. Yet, because of this we see a lack of understanding of the uses of money in an increasing tendency of the society towards gambling, borrowing and not paying back, and stealing. For the Christian and Jewish believer our finances should be committed to God.

We can also look at coinage and see the history of the Bible being revealed to us. Coins reveal to us that there was a Caesar Augustus during the time that Jesus was born. The denarius of Tiberius was probably used by Jesus as a teaching tool, as well as the "widow's mite" to instruct people. The denarius was used to instruct the people about submission to the leaders of the land, "render unto Caesar the things that are Caesar's", and the "widow's mite" on what the attitude of giving should be. As the scriptures state, she gave all she had into the Temple treasury, and yet Jesus proclaimed that she had given more than all the others.

Coins reveal to us the progression of nations as described in the Book of Daniel. We have concrete substance in the Persian Siglos, which gave way to the Greek Stater, then the Roman denarius, and now the rise of the European Union Euro coin. And just as Jesus came in the fullness of time during the rule of Caesar Augustus, when there was common coinage and a unified Roman Empire under one man so a man will arise to lead the renewed Roman Empire: the anti-Christ. Coinage is being produced as a fulfillment of the prophecy. The scriptures also proclaim Jesus will come a second time as the Messiah who will save His people the Jews, and the Christians who have believed in Him.

This then brings us to the point of the value of studying coins in history. The Holy Scriptures teach that if a man gains the "whole world", becomes very wealthy, yet loses his soul then he has gained nothing and lost everything. The Bible also says that all the works of man, done by him to justify himself, are as "filthy rags" before the Lord (Isaiah 64:6). So no man can save himself, or please God, by his own works. Because of this dilemma many through the ages have cried out to God "what must I do to be saved?" See (Acts 16:30). The scriptures give a clear answer.

The Holy Scriptures, Judeo-Christian, proclaim throughout its writings that God would send a Messiah who would suffer and die for man's sins. It says in Isaiah (53:1-12) that He would be crushed for iniquities and chastened for our well-being.[298] It talks about Jesus having been nailed to a cross for the sins of men. In Zechariah (12:10; and John 19:17) the prophet says that the Jewish people in the Last Days would look upon Him whom they pierced as an only son; and in that day they would repent as a nation to accept Him as the Messiah. This has yet to occur.

Jesus Christ, who was sinless, was made (chose) to bear the sins of men. In the book of Romans its says, "whoever will call upon the name of the Lord will be saved." "If you confess with your mouth Jesus *as* Lord, and believe in your heart that God raised Him from the dead, you will be saved" (or delivered from eternal punishment). It says, "for with the heart a person believes, resulting in righteousness, and with the mouth he confesses, resulting in salvation" (Romans 10:1-13). Also, in the book of Joshua (24:15) it says "choose this day whom you will serve".

Coins are just another source of verification of the veracity of the Holy Bible. Therefore, let us act upon the principles of these Holy Scriptures.

---

[298] **Isaiah 53:**1 "Who has believed our message? And to whom has the arm of the Lord been revealed? ²For He grew up before Him like a tender shoot, and like a root out of parched ground; He has no *stately* form or majesty that we should look upon Him, nor appearance that we should be attracted to Him. ³He was despised and forsaken of men, a man of sorrows and acquainted with grief; and like one from whom men hide their face. He was despised, and we did not esteem Him. ⁴Surely our griefs He Himself bore, and our sorrows He carried; yet we ourselves esteemed Him stricken, smitten of God, and afflicted. ⁵But He was pierced through for our transgressions, He was crushed for our iniquities; the chastening for our well-being *fell* upon Him, and by His scourging we are healed. ⁶All of us like sheep have gone astray, each of us has turned to his own way; but the Lord has caused the iniquity of us all to fall on Him. ⁷He was oppressed and He was afflicted, yet He did not open His mouth; like a lamb that is led to slaughter, and like a sheep that is silent before its shearers, so He did not open His mouth. ⁸By oppression and judgment He was taken away; and as for His generation, who considered that He was cut off out of the land of the living for the transgression of my people, to whom the stroke *was due*? ⁹His grave was assigned with wicked men, yet He was with a rich man in His death, because He had done no violence, nor was there any deceit in His mouth. ¹⁰But the Lord was pleased to crush Him, putting *Him* to grief; if He would render Himself *as* a guilt offering, He will see *His* offspring, He will prolong *His* days, and the good pleasure of the Lord will prosper in His hand. ¹¹As a result of the anguish of His soul, He will see *it and* be satisfied; by His knowledge the Righteous One, My Servant, will justify the many, as He will bear their iniquities. ¹²Therefore, I will allot Him a portion with the great, and He will divide the booty with the strong; because He poured out Himself to death, and was numbered with the transgressors; yet He Himself bore the sin of many, and interceded for the transgressors."

BIBLIOGRAPHY

1) Arab Islamic Coins, online Forumancient.com.

2) Doty, Richard G. Money of the World, 1978. Grosset and Dunlap inc.

3) Eusebius: The History of the Church from Christ to Constantine, translated by GA Williamson, New York University Press, New York, NY, 1965.

4) Gilbert, Martin. Israel, Harper Perennial, New York, NY, first published by Doubleday Great Britain, 1998, reprint 2008.

5) Grant Michael. The Twelve Caesars, Barnes and Noble, New York, NY, 1975.

6) Grayzel, Solomon. A History of the Jews, The Jewish Publication Society of America, Philadelphia, PA, 1947.

7) Haffner, S. The History of Modern Israel's Money (HMIM), 1967. San Diego, CA.

8) Hendin, D. Guide to Biblical Coins, 1st Ed. 1987. Amphora Books, NY.

9) Hendin, D. Guide to Biblical Coins, 4th Ed. 2001. Amphora Books, NY.

10) Hendin, David Ancient Scale Weights, 2007. Amphora, Nyack, NY.

11) Holy Bible. online public domain.

12) Josephus Complete Works, translated by William Whiston, Kregel Publications, Grand Rapids, MI, 1960.

13) Kac, Arthur. The Rebirth of the State of Israel, Moody Press, Chicago, Il, 1958.

14) Kauffman, J. Chaim Unrecorded Hasmonean Coins from the J. Chaim Kaufman Collection, 2004. Publications of the Israel Numismatic Society, Vol X, Graphit Press Ltd, Jerusalem.

15) Larkin, Clarence. The Book of Daniel, Clarence Larkin Est. Philadephia, PA, 1929. (author died 1924)

16) Larkin, Clarence. Book of Revelation, Clarence Larkin Est. Philadelphia, PA, 1929.

17) Leslie, John G. The Noah Flood Account – A True Narrative Representation, Trinity Southwest University Press (in press).

18) Meshorer, Ya'akov and Shraga Qedar Samarian Coinage, 1999. The Israel Numismatic Society, Graphit Press Ltd, Jerusalem.

19) Meshorer, Ya'akov Testimoney, 2000. The Israel Museum, Jerusalem.

20) Meshorer, Ya'akov A Treasury of Jewish Coins, 2001. Yad Ben-Zvi Press, Jerusalem and Amphora, Nyack, NY.

21) Nastich, Vladimir N. A Survey of Abbasid Copper Coinage of Transoxiana, date uncertain. Online: http://www.charm.ru/info/library/Nastich/Nastich=Abbasid%20AE%20Coinage%20of%20Transoxiana.pdf

22) Reich, Ronny. Excavating the City of David: Where Jerusalem's History Began, Israel Exploration Society, IS, 2014.

23) Ritmeyer, Leen. The Quest: Revealing the Temple Mount in Jerusalem, Carta Publishing, IS, 2012.

24) Sear, D.R. Greek Coins and their values, Vol. 2 Asia and Africa, 1979. Robert Stockwell Ltd, London.

25) The American Numismatic Society Syllogue Nummorum Graecorum, Part 6 Palestine-South Arabia, 1981. Printed by Meriden Gravure Co., Meriden, Conn.

26) Tacitus: The Complete Works, translated by Alfred Church and William Jacob Brodribb, The Modern Library, New York, NY, 1942.

27) The Newadvent.org (A Catholic encyclopedia online-a good resource on general Christian information.)

28) Van Mater, D. The Handbook of Roman Imperial Coins, 1991 reprint 2000. Laurion Press, Utica, NY.

29) Yadin, Yigael. Masada. Random House, New York, NY, 1966.

30) www.JewishVirtual Library.org.

Appendices   Page

1) Coin Stamping, cut coins, co-stamps of Roman Legions on coins   122

2) Coin Identification of Roman, Greek, and Jewish coins   124

3) Prutah vs. Lepta   125

4) Use of coins in the identifying of archaeological sites: 126
   Bethsaida, Masada, Jerusalem ancient sewer, coin mints found in Israel

5) Roman Noah's Ark Coin   130

5) Ptolemy Coin Hoard   132

6) The Maji - Who Were They?   133

7) The Samaritans - Who Were They?   134

8) True/false religions portrayed in coins   144

9) The Orphic Egg in Greek and Roman Societies vs. the Jewish Holy God   146

10) Smelting processes   148

11) Raw materials for smelting or hammering   149

12) Electrum coins and other items   150

13) Clay forger's mold   151

14) Scripture Relating to the Messiah   152

15) He is Risen   153

Jewish Coin Counter in 1910

Legend for Coin Stamping

(Coin stamps of Roman Legions on other coins, cut coins as denominations.)

1) **Multiple stamped coins**:

Purpose: used to identify authentic vs. fake coins, and as barter marks in certain regions.

Ex. Persian Siglos (note some fake coins were silver plated with copper cores which could be detected by counter-stamping)

2) **Roman Legions: Stamps** were used to identify control over certain regions.

- left side the Roman numeral for ten and the 10th Legion "boar".

-right side 12th Legion "Fulminata" (defeated by Bar Kochba)

3) **Cut Coins**

Purpose: as coins were in somewhat short supply, perhaps fractions of value for commercial reasons could be obtained by cutting coins.

-used as fractions of coins

-left ex. Of denarius (cut silver) Caracalla

-right bronze of Augustus

Cut Coins Fractions and Multiple Stamp Coins

(coins not to relative size)

Ancient Coin Identification
Roman, Greek, Jewish

ROMAN

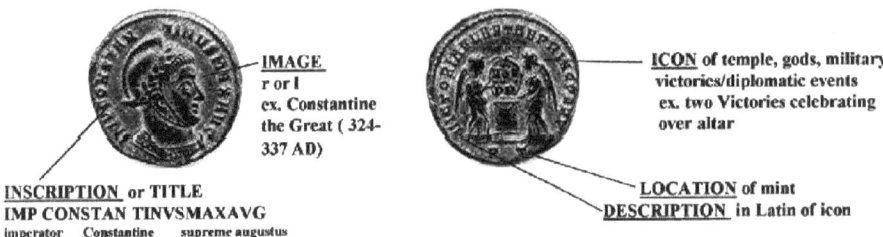

IMAGE
r or l
ex. Constantine the Great (324-337 AD)

INSCRIPTION or TITLE
IMP CONSTAN TINVSMAXAVG
imperator   Constantine   supreme augustus

ICON of temple, gods, military victories/diplomatic events
ex. two Victories celebrating over altar

LOCATION of mint
DESCRIPTION in Latin of icon

GREEK

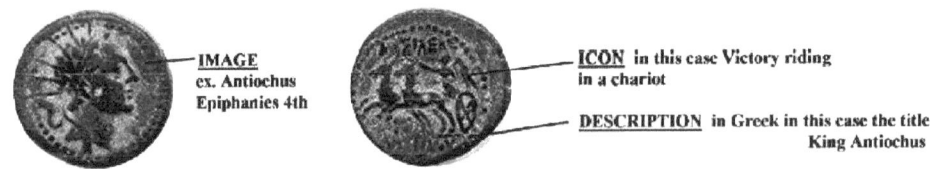

IMAGE
ex. Antiochus Epiphanies 4th

ICON in this case Victory riding in a chariot

DESCRIPTION in Greek in this case the title King Antiochus

JEWISH

OBVERSE (FRONT)
Hasmonean (Maccabbean)
No image of man or beast allowed

REVERSE (BACK)
written in archaic (paleo) Hebrew saying "John the High Priest and the Council of the Jews"

BAR KOCHBA COIN
archaic Hebrew
ש ש ם ס ↑ y
read r to l
y ↑ ס ם ש ש
in English Shimon Bar Kochba's 1st name
Palm Tree Motif on both Old and Modern coins

MODERN
Hebrew Block Letter
Arabic Script
Mint Date
1949-55

Jewish Prutah and Lepta

Lepta

"How much was the widow's mite?

We find the story of the widow's mite in Mark 12:41-44 and Luke 21:1-4…The Greek text in Mark 12:42 says that she dropped in 'two lepta, which is a kodrantes.' …But in the first century, a kodrantes was equal to 1/64 of a denarius, and a denarius was considered fair pay for a day's wage. If today's wage for a laborer in the USA is $15 per hour, that comes to $120 for an 8-hour day. At this rate, 1/64 of a day's wage is $1.88. Round it up to $2.00, and we could say that the widow dropped two dollar-coins into the collection box. That feels very different from 'two coins worth only a fraction of a penny.'…the point of Jesus' teaching was that the widow gave everything she had. And if her two small coins were worth a couple of dollars in our economy, let's not give the impression that she had only two pennies. …"

http://www.nltblog.com/index.php/2010/04/how-much-was-the-widows-mite/

Prutah

"Prutah (Hebrew: פרוטה) is a word borrowed from the Mishnah and the Talmud, in which it means "a coin of smaller value". The word was probably derived originally from an Aramaic word with the same meaning. The prutah was an ancient copper Jewish coin worth about one thousandth of a pound. A loaf of bread at that time was worth about 10 prutot (plural of prutah). One prutah was also worth two lepta (singular lepton), which was the smallest denomination minted by the Hasmonean and Herodian Dynasty kings. Prutot were also minted by the Roman Procurators of the Province of Judea, and later were minted by the Jews during the First Jewish Revolt (sometimes called 'Masada coins')."

https://en.wikipedia.org/wiki/Prutah

Prutah and Lepta
(Size of Coins)

1.5 cm

Bethsaida
Coins Used to Document Occupation

There have been over 600 coins found at the Bibical site if Bethsaida. They range from the Greek Classic/Helenistic Periods, Ptolemaic, Seleucid, Hasmonean, Herodian to Early/Late Roman. The Byzantine Period is sparcely represented; but the Islamic Periods are present. Umayyad, Abbasid, Fatimid coins have been found. Then a few Crusader coins are present followed by later Islamic periods: Mamluk and early Ottoman. The author of this study then designates the late Ottoman Period, European and Syrian coins as modern. The coins found were minted in a diverse number of mints including: Ako-Ptolemaic, Alexandria, Antioch(Syria), Damascus, Egypt, Jerusalem, Rome, Tiberius, Tyre and others. About one half of the coins are from undentified mints. He summarizes the finds as follows:
- there is a clear transition of Ptolomaic to Seleucid to Hasmonean rule in the coins,
-early Roman is found at the site from about 0-200 AD,
-it appears that the site was aboandoned for 1000 years afterwards,
-in 1220 AD some Islamic coins are seen in the area, but the number of coins increased significantly in the Late Ottoman Period, although many of the later coins were pierced and thus may have been used for jewelry rather than commerce.Information taken from:
Gregory Jenks: **www.academia.edu/11316665/The_Coins_from_Bethsaida**
Coins similar to ones at the site(except Islamic one): **www.biblewalks.com/Sites/BethsaidaCoins.html**

Map 1911 public domain

Gateway to Bethsaida

Alexander the Great 356-323 BC

Herod Antipas 20 BC-39 AD

Herod Agrippa II 27 AD-92 AD

Marcus Julius Philippus ("Philip the Arab") 204-249 AD

Islamic: Ottoman uncertain of date or mint

MASADA
AND THE USE OF COINS IN ARCHEOLOGY

From the writings of Josephus, the tragic last stand of Jewish resistance (of the rebellion) took place at Masada in 74 A.D. This butte fortress of Herod the Great fell to the Romans, but not before 960 Jewish men, women, and children committed suicide. The last of the resistors torched the buildings (and possibly the Romans did so as well). Certain coins have been identified in the ashen remains of this event (see coin 1 under Jewish War). These coins were found scattered around in the ash on the floors of the storage buildings. The association of these coins with this written historical event allowed them to be used in helping to identify other archeology sites of the period.

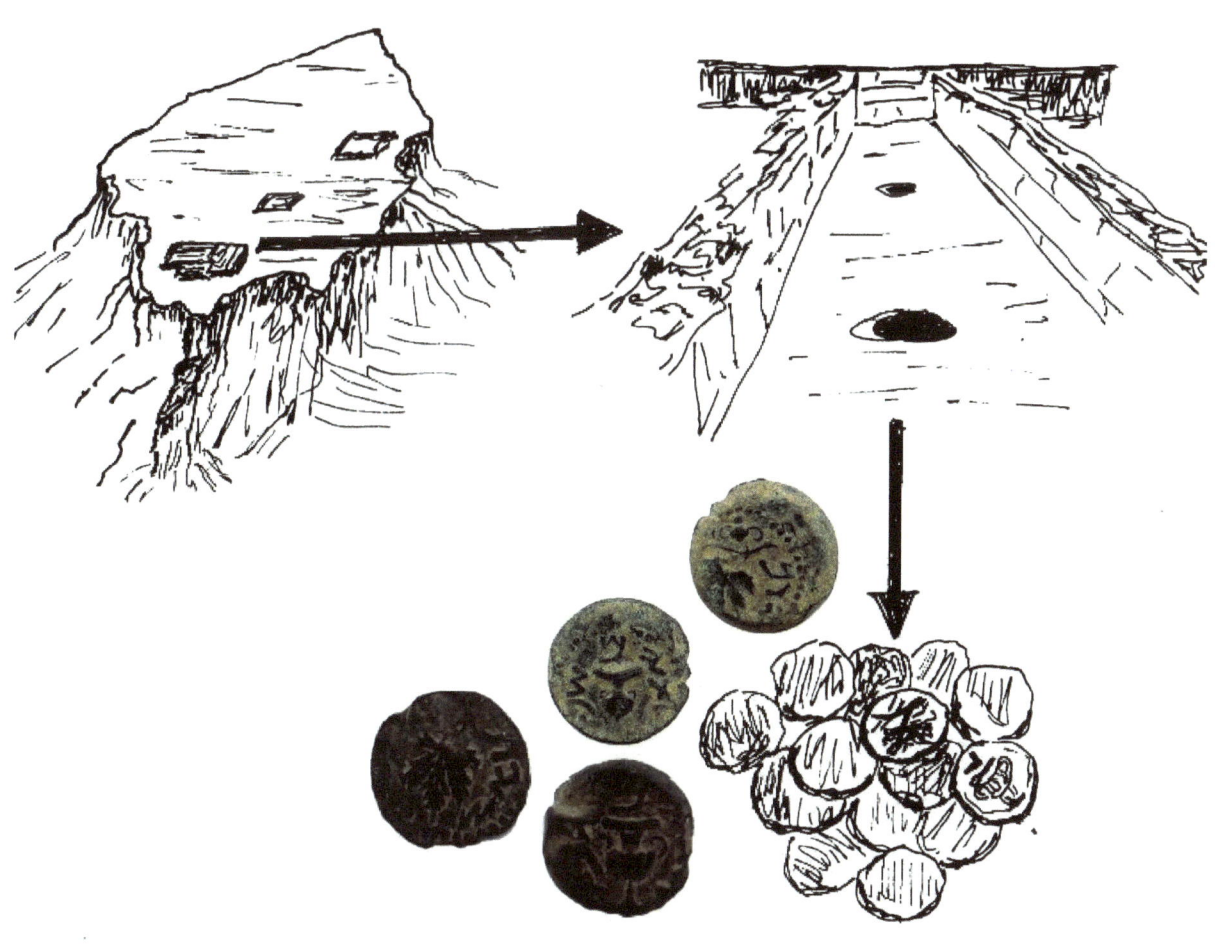

Jerusalem Sewage System
Dated Approximately by a Coin 70 AD

Tyrian tetradrachm like one found in the sewage tunnel. Only accepted coin, because of its purity of silver, for the Temple Tax. (Data see Ronny Reich: Excavating the City of David)

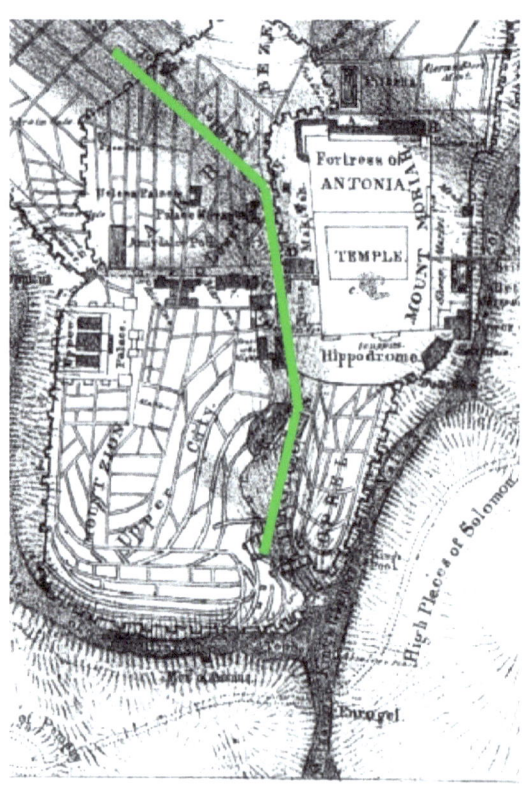

ANCIENT JERUSALEM.

Sewage Tunnel Running along the west side of the Temple Mount in the Tyropoeon Valley
(See green line. Map Barkely 1800's, postion of tunnel from Leen Ritmeyer: The Quest)

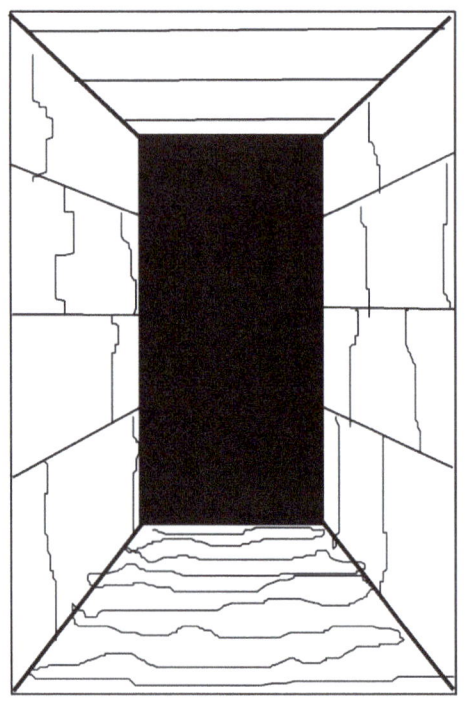

Jerusalem Sewage Tunnel Lined with processed Stone - a man can stand upright in it.

Ancient Coin Mints (some) Placed on Map from 1711 of Caanan

(see D Hendin *Biblical Coins*)

Roman Noah's Ark Coin

PHRYGIA, Apameia (Kibotos). *Philip I.* AD 244-249. Æ Medallion (34mm, 22.02 g, 6h). M. Aurelius Alexandros II, *archiereus* (high priest).[299]

"These famous 'Noah' coins were issued in the city of Apameia, Phrygia, in the 3rd century AD, when the city was under Roman rule, and some of them were struck by city officials who were Jewish. The Noah coin design must have been very popular because it was struck for the emperors Septimius Severus, AD 192-211, Severus Alexander, 222-235, Gordian III, 238-244, Philip 1, 244-249, and Trebonianus Callus, 251-253, over a period of 61 years."[300]

It should be noted that secular cultures throughout the world and time have had histories of a worldwide Flood[301]. This event was acknowledged on the Roman coins of Phrygia. As has been noted throughout this book coins were used to promote a king, place, or event. The Jewish Account of the Noah Flood was prominent in both secular and Jewish cultures.[297]

---

[299] https://cngcoins.com/Coins.aspx?CATEGORY_ID=115&VIEW_TYPE=0
[300] http://www.theshekel.org/article_noahs_ark.html
[301] Every continent on the face of the earth, except possibly Antarctica, has Flood stories that are ancient in context. See www.DefendingtheChristianFaith.org. I have attached my dissertation on the subject on that website.

Noah's Ark Coin: People in Ancient Times Believed the Jewish Accounts as History

PHRYGIA, Apamea. Gordian III. 238-244 A.D. Æ 39mm 27.51g. Noah and wife in arc (right); Noah and wife on dry land post-flood with dove above (left) SNG von Aulock 8347 (image courtesy of CNG/Triton V). Permit to use coin image from Classic Numistmatic Group 6-20-16: cng@cngcoins.com

Ptolemy Coin Hoard

Coin hoards are common. Above is a partial sample of a hoard (75 total) of Ptolomy coins. Some of the coins are quite corroded. They can be markers of the destruction of a city or area. Many other examples exist:

"Egyptian Minister of Culture Farouk Hosni announced today the discovery of 383 coins from the Ptolemaic period in the Fayum, or Faiyum, Oasis...According to the statement released by the SCA (Supreme Council of Antiquities) the coinage, very well preserved and dating to the reign of King Ptolemy III (243 to 222BC), was discovered during routine excavations north of Lake Quarun...Dr. Zahi Hawass, Secretary General of the SCA, said that the 383 coins are fashioned out of bronze and have a weight of 32 grams each. They are decorated on one side with a scene depicting the god Amon-Zeus (Amon was identified by the Greeks as a form of Zeus), with two horns and a cobra. The other side of the coin is decorated with a falcon standing on a wooden branch. Underneath, 'King Ptolemy' is written in Greek." http://www.independent.co.uk/ 10-23-2011

"In February of 1948 a group of 34 bronze coins of the Ptolemaic period was found during the excavation of a well in the South Stoa of Corinth. Although no container was in evidence, the circumstances of the finding indicate that this is a hoard whose final burial is to be related to the destruction of the city in 146 B.C."
www.ascsa.edu.gr/pdf/uploads/hesperia/146804.pdf

Who Were the Magi?

"After Jesus was born in Bethlehem in Judea, during the time of King Herod, Magi from the east came to Jerusalem and asked, 'Where is the one who has been born king of the Jews? We saw his star in the east and have come to worship him.'" (Matthew 2:1-2)

1. **Parthia or Persia.** The term *magoi* was first associated with the Medes and the Persians. We know that astrology flourished in this area and that the astral lore of the region was applied to royal births. (Ex. Phraates V ruled Media from 2 BC-4 AD.)

2. **Babylon.** The Babylonians or Chaldeans had a well developed interest in astronomy and astrology. A large colony of Jews remained there, so astrologers could have learned of Jewish messianic expectations. Also, *magoi* are referred to in Daniel's description of the Babylonian court. (Azes 2 was King of Bactria, north of Babylon, from 35 BC-5AD. It was home to the Zoroastrians. Hermaios was King in Bactria 90-70 BC, but his coins were posthumous struck by Kadphises 30-80 AD)[302] These may have been disciples of Daniel the prophet who had resided in Babylon. As such they could have been Jewish astronomers that remained in Babylon generation upon generation waiting for signs in the Heavens declaring the coming of the Messiah.

3. **Arabia or the Syrian Desert.** The gifts of gold, frankincense, and myrrh are associated with desert camel trains coming from Midian in northwest Arabia or Sheba in southwest Arabia. Astrology was not unknown and Jewish colonies existed in various cities."[303] Others feel they may have been from as far away as **China**, and they arrived months after He (Y'shua or Jesus) had been born.[304]

Coins of Leaders of Eastern Countries About the Time of Christ That May Reflect the Magi

Phraates V, Hermaios, Azes 2

---

[302] http://www.wildwinds.com/coins/greece/baktria/kings/hermaios/.
[303] http://www.jesuswalk.com/christmas-incarnation/magi-star.htm Inserts by JGL.
[304] http://www.biblicalarchaeology.org/daily/people-cultures-in-the-bible/jesus-historical-jesus/bible-scholar-brent-landau-asks-%E2%80%9Cwho-were-the-magi%E2%80%9D/. He reviewed and translated a Syriac, from the Vatican, manuscript dated to the 700's AD. The earliest copies may have done about 200 AD.

Who Were the Samaritans?

Samaria, the area north and northwest of Jerusalem, played an important part in the history of the Jewish people. A brief history of the people groups of this area and their impact on the Jewish people will be discussed here along with representative coins. A timeline is below:

3000 BC (approximate) Area is inhabited by the Canaanites post Flood.

Genesis 10:15 Canaan became the father of Sidon, his firstborn, and Heth [16] and the Jebusite and the Amorite and the Girgashite [17] and the Hivite and the Arkite and the Sinite [18] and the Arvadite and the Zemarite and the Hamathite; and afterward the families of the Canaanite were spread abroad. [19] The territory of the Canaanite extended from Sidon as you go toward Gerar, as far as Gaza; as you go toward Sodom and Gomorrah and Admah and Zeboiim, as far as Lasha.

2000 BC (approximately 1800 BC) Area was given by promise (covenant) to Abraham.

Genesis 15:18 On that day the LORD made a covenant with Abram, saying, "To your descendants I have given this land, from the river of Egypt as far as the great river, the river Euphrates: [19] the Kenite and the Kenizzite and the Kadmonite [20] and the Hittite and the Perizzite and the Rephaim [21] and the Amorite and the Canaanite and the Girgashite and the Jebusite."

In this same incident God tells Abram (renamed Abraham after the covenant) that his offspring would be taken out of the land for a period of time. The reason:

Genesis 15:16 "Then in the fourth generation they will return here, for the iniquity of the Amorite is not yet complete.

1450 BC Joshua would lead the Jewish people back into the land promised by God to Abraham, after the "inquity" of the Amorites had become full-and God judged them.

Joshua 1:1 Now it came about after the death of Moses the servant of the LORD, that the LORD spoke to Joshua the son of Nun, Moses' servant, saying, [2] "Moses My servant is dead; now therefore arise, cross this Jordan, you and all this people, to the land which I am giving to them, to the sons of Israel. [3] Every place on which the sole of your foot treads, I have given it to you, just as I spoke to Moses. [4] From the wilderness and this Lebanon, even as far as the great river, the river Euphrates, all the land of the Hittites, and as far as the Great Sea toward the setting of the sun will be your territory.

Please note that the land was never fully conquered by the Jewish peoples, and the people groups left behind would become a "thorn in their sides and eyes".

This is seen as Joshua on his death bed spoke to the Jewish people.

Joshua 23:6 Be very firm, then, to keep and do all that is written in the book of the law of Moses, so that you may not turn aside from it to the right hand or to the left, [7] so that you will not associate with these nations, these which remain among you, or mention the name of their gods, or make *anyone* swear *by them*, or serve them, or bow down to them. [8] But you are to cling to the LORD your God, as you have done to this day. [9] For the LORD has driven out great and strong nations from before you; and as for you, no man has stood before you to this day. [10] One of your men puts to flight a thousand, for the LORD your God is He who fights for you, just as He promised you. [11] So take diligent heed to yourselves to love the LORD your God. **[12] For if you ever go back and cling to the rest of these nations, these which remain among you, and intermarry with them, so that you associate with them and they with you, [13] know with certainty that the LORD your God will not continue to drive these nations out from before you; but they will be a snare and a trap to you, and a whip on your sides and thorns in your eyes, until you perish from off this good land which the LORD your God has given you.**

The area of Samaria was given to Joseph's clan when the land was being divided among the Jewish tribes.

1000 BC Solomon died in 931 BC and the 10 northern tribes were separated from the 2 southern ones. About 884 BC Omri built the capital Shomron in Samara and expanded the northern tribe holdings along the east side of the Jordan to Moab. (I Kings 16:24)

744 BC[305] Not much documentation has been left till Tigath-Pileser III invaded the northern area in 744 BC. He moved most of the ten tribes to the east (Assyria) and replaced them with a people group from there, Cuthaeans. Shalmeneser V (Assyria) invaded Canaan in 726 BC. From this point on the Jews left behind in Samaria intermarried and took on the polytheism of the new groups.[306, 307] The reason for the captivity from a Biblical perspective was:

Judges 18:30 The sons of Dan set up for themselves the graven image; and Jonathan, the son of Gershom, the son of Manasseh, he and his sons were priests to the tribe of the Danites until the day of the captivity of the land. ³¹ So they set up for themselves Micah's graven image which he had made, all the time that the house of God was at Shiloh.

This was a direct violation of the 1st and 2nd Commandments that Moses had given the Jewish people in Exodus 34.

612-605 BC The Babylonians overthrew the Assyrians and the Egyptians at the Battle of Carchemish:

"The Battle of Carchemish was fought in May/June of 605 BC between an allied army of Egyptians and Assyrians against the Babylonian army. When the Assyrian capital of Ninevah was overrun by the Babylonians in 612 BC, the Assyrians moved their capital to Harran (now in Turkey). When the Babylonians captured Harran in 608 BC, the Assyrian capital was moved to Carchemish. Egypt was allied with the Assyrians, and marched to their aid against the Babylonians."[308]

587 BC Nebuchadnezzar captured Jerusalem.[309] The Jews from the southern tribes, Judah and Benjamin, were taken into captivity for their iniquity as the prophet Jeremiah stated:

Jeremiah 25:11 This whole land will be a desolation and a horror, and these nations will serve the king of Babylon seventy years. ¹² 'Then it will be when seventy years are completed I will punish the king of Babylon and that nation,' declares the LORD, 'for their iniquity, and the land of the Chaldeans; and I will make it an everlasting desolation.

Jeremiah 25:1 The word that came to Jeremiah concerning all the people of Judah, in the fourth year of Jehoiakim the son of Josiah, king of Judah (that was the first year of Nebuchadnezzar king of Babylon), ²which Jeremiah the prophet spoke to all the people of Judah and to all the inhabitants of Jerusalem, saying, ³"From the thirteenth year of Josiah the son of Amon, king of Judah, even to this day, these twenty-three years the word of the LORD has come to me, and I have spoken to you again and again, but you have not listened. ⁴And the LORD has sent to you all His servants the prophets again and

---

[305] 2 Kings 15:29 "In the days of Pekah king of Israel came Tiglathpileser king of Assyria, and took Ijon, and Abelbethmaachah, and Janoah, and Kedesh, and Hazor, and Gilead, and Galilee, all the land of Naphtali, and carried them captive to Assyria."
[306] There are some documentations: ostracons, names of leaders etc. that indicate that many of those left behind tried to maintain their Jewish identity. But, the returning Jews from Babylon would eventually reject them. As such they began to worship Yahweh at Mt. Gerizim instead of at Jerusalem. Y. Meshorer and S. Qedar, 1999, Samarian Coinage, pg. 11.
[307] There is a cuneiform tablet that documents the area of Samaria having to pay a grain tax to Nabu-duru-usur in Assyria in 710 B.C. From: Younger, K. Lawson Jr. "A Letter Concerning the Grain Tax of the Samarians (3-97)." In *Context of Scripture Online*. Editor in Chief: W..Hallo. Brill Online, 2015.
[308] http://www.padfield.com/2008/carchemish.html
[309] He combined the areas of Samaria and Jerusalem together. See Livius.org.

again, but you have not listened nor inclined your ear to hear, ⁵saying, 'Turn now everyone from his evil way and from the evil of your deeds, and dwell on the land which the LORD has given to you and your forefathers forever and ever; ⁶and do not go after other gods to serve them and to worship them, and do not provoke Me to anger with the work of your hands, and I will do you no harm.'⁷Yet you have not listened to Me," declares the LORD, "in order that you might provoke Me to anger with the work of your hands to your own harm. ⁸"Therefore thus says the LORD of hosts, 'Because you have not obeyed My words, ⁹behold, I will send and take all the families of the north,' declares the LORD, 'and *I will send* to Nebuchadnezzar king of Babylon, My servant, and will bring them against this land and against its inhabitants and against all these nations round about; and I will utterly destroy them and make them a horror and a hissing, and an everlasting desolation.

2 Kings 24:1 In his days Nebuchadnezzar king of Babylon came up, and Jehoiakim became his servant *for* three years; then he turned and rebelled against him. ²The LORD sent against him bands of Chaldeans, bands of Arameans, bands of Moabites, and bands of Ammonites. So He sent them against Judah to destroy it, according to the word of the LORD which He had spoken through His servants the prophets. ³Surely at the command of the LORD it came upon Judah, to remove *them* from His sight because of the sins of Manasseh, according to all that he had done,⁴and also for the innocent blood which he shed, for he filled Jerusalem with innocent blood; and the LORD would not forgive. ⁵Now the rest of the acts of Jehoiakim and all that he did, are they not written in the Book of the Chronicles of the Kings of Judah?

559 BC Cyrus captured Babylon and released people groups back to their lands. It had been seventy years as prophesied by Jeremiah. As well, he facilitated the building of the Jewish Temple:

Ezra 1:1 Now in the first year of Cyrus king of Persia, in order to fulfill the word of the LORD by the mouth of Jeremiah, the LORD stirred up the spirit of Cyrus king of Persia, so that he sent a proclamation throughout all his kingdom, and also *put it* in writing, saying: ²"Thus says Cyrus king of Persia, 'The LORD, the God of heaven, has given me all the kingdoms of the earth and He has appointed me to build Him a house in Jerusalem, which is in Judah. ³Whoever there is among you of all His people, may his God be with him! Let him go up to Jerusalem which is in Judah and rebuild the house of the LORD, the God of Israel; He is the God who is in Jerusalem.

Samaritans, who had been left behind during the captivity of the Northern Tribes as well as other groups, remained submitted/committed to the Persians, and were able to mint coins. (See coin 1 of Phoenicia-Sidon in the Samaritan Coin Figures). Coins would also be minted in Jerusalem, once Jews from the southern tribes returned, with approval from the Persians, under the designation of YHD (Judah-see main text).[310]

332 BC Alexander the Great overthrew the Persian government. He assisted Sanballat, who opposed a Temple in Jerusalem,[311] and who had requested a temple on Mt. Gerizim. The Samaritans would have their own text version of the mount where Abraham would have considered sacrificing Isaac.[312, 313]

---

[310] D. Hendin, 1984, Guide to Biblical Coins, pg. 33-38. "During the Persian period coins were used and struck for the first time in the land of Israel. See section on Persian coins in the main text.

[311] Nehemiah 4:1 Now it came about that when Sanballat heard that we were rebuilding the wall, he became furious and very angry and mocked the Jews. ²He spoke in the presence of his brothers and the wealthy *men* of Samaria and said, "What are these feeble Jews doing?

[312] Authors at Livius.org comment: "We can probably be a bit more precise about the moment when the Torah was introduced in the north. In the 330's, there was discord among the priests of Jerusalem, and several members of this order left the city. They settled in Samaria, and in 332, they were able to get permission from the Macedonian conqueror Alexander the Great to build a temple near Shechem on Mount Gerizim…Archeology has more or less confirmed this story, which is told by Flavius Josephus…But the temple of Shechem was close to Jerusalem and challenged the latter's position as the one and

321 BC Seleucids gained control of the area. Seleucus, one of Alexander's leading generals, became satrap (governor) of Babylonia in 321 BC, two years after the death of Alexander. From this group would come Antiochus IV. "Antiochus IV Epiphanes, (Greek: "God Manifest") also called Antiochus Epiphanes (the Mad) (born *c.* 215 BC-died 164, Tabae, Iran), Seleucid king of the Hellenistic Syrian kingdom who reigned from 175 to 164 BC. As a ruler he was best known for his encouragement of Greek culture and institutions."[314] He attempted to sacrifice a swine on the Temple area of Jerusalem. This led to the Maccabean Revolt.[315] Coins from this period have been found in the area of Samaria which has confirmed the presence of Greek influence in the area during this period. (See coin 2, 3 Athena/Owl in the Samaritan Coin Figures.)

164(5) BC John Hyrcanus (134-104 BC), as leader of the Maccabeans, invaded and destroyed the temple at Mt. Gerizim. He required that all Jews north and south worship at the temple in Jerusalem. This created a persisting animosity with the Samarians Jews.

63 BC Pompey, the Roman general, entered and captured Jerusalem. Northern and southern Jewish communities became separated.

31 BC Octavian (Augustus) combined the northern and southern Jewish peoples.[316]

6 AD Judea was made a province of Rome. Samaria and Jerusalem remained linked. In the gospels Jesus and the disciples did go through Samaria and converts to Christianity occurred. (Example: the story of the woman at the well.)

Acts 8:14 Now when the apostles in Jerusalem heard that Samaria had received the word of God, they sent them Peter and John, ¹⁵who came down and prayed for them that they might receive the Holy Spirit. ¹⁶For He had not yet fallen upon any of them; they had simply been baptized in the name of the Lord Jesus. ¹⁷Then they *began* laying their hands on them, and they were receiving the Holy Spirit.

65-70 AD The Jewish Wars. Sebaste, the northern capital, was destroyed by Jews from the south when they rebelled against the Roman government. It was later rebuilt and renamed as Neapolis by the Romans. In 70 AD the Jewish Temple, in Jerusalem, was torn down by the Romans. (See notes in main text.) Yet, Mt. Gerizim, where the Samaritans worshipped, remained (although the temple was destroyed) as a place of worship. Roman coins even into the 3rd Century contained images of Mount

---

only shrine of YHWH. From now on the two groups were to grow apart…The city of Samaria, more cosmopolitan than Jerusalem, was inhabited by several groups of pagans, and their cult practices may have influenced those of their YHWH-worshipping fellow-citizens." http://www.livius.org/articles/people/samaritans/.

[313] Jesus would rebuke them for this belief: John 4: ¹⁹ The woman said to Him, "Sir, I perceive that You are a prophet.²⁰ Our fathers worshiped in this mountain, and you *people* say that in Jerusalem is the place where men ought to worship." ²¹ Jesus said to her, "Woman, believe Me, an hour is coming when neither in this mountain nor in Jerusalem will you worship the Father. ²² You worship what you do not know; we worship what we know, for salvation is from the Jews. ²³ But an hour is coming, and now is, when the true worshipers will worship the Father in spirit and truth; for such people the Father seeks to be His worshipers."

[314] http://www.britannica.com/biography/Antiochus-IV-Epiphanes

[315] "The Greeks and those friendly toward them were united into the community of Antiochians; the worship of Yahweh and all of the Jewish rites were forbidden on pain of death. In the Temple an altar to Zeus Olympios was erected, and sacrifices were to be made at the feet of an idol in the image of the King. Against that desecration Judas Maccabeus, leader of the anti-Greek Jews, led the aroused Hasideans in a guerrilla war and several times defeated the generals Antiochus had commissioned to deal with the uprising. Judas refused a partial amnesty, conquered Judaea with the exception of the Acra in Jerusalem, and in December 164 was able to tear down the altar of Zeus and re-consecrate the Temple." Antiochus would die of an illness before he could return to Israel. http://www.britannica.com/biography/Antiochus-IV-Epiphanes.

[316] Livius.org.

Gerizim and its temple.[317] (See coin 3 of Alexander Severus dated about 238 AD in Samaritan Coin Figures.)

132 AD Bar Kochba Rebellion. Jews were disbanded and prohibited from returning to the city of Jerusalem. See notes on Bar Kochba in main text.

578 AD The Samaritans revolted against Roman/Byzantine rule. They were crushed by Justinian.[318]

600-700 AD[319] Mohammed was born about 570 AD and proclaimed that he was the final prophet from God.[320] His writings allowed for the conquering of the lands of "unbelievers" and by 638 AD his influence through followers had been forcefully spread into Judea and Samaria.[321,322]

1000-1200 AD During this period there were repetitive conflicts between Crusader groups and Islamic groups over Jerusalem. Saladin finally defeated the Crusaders at the battle of Hattin.[323] They recovered some of the lands in the 3rd Crusade.[324] And then they became dissipated and involuted upon themselves during the 4th Crusade.[325]

---

[317] Ibid Livius.org. Samaritans. The Romans seemed to have accepted worship at Mt. Gerizim but not Jerusalem.
[318] Ibid. The authors comment that this defeat and the rise of Islam probably caused the significant decrease in the population of the Samaritans.
[319] https://en.wikipedia.org/wiki/Muhammad
[320] "The Quran teaches that Muhammad is the seal of the prophets, with the implication being that he is the last prophet: 'Muhammad is not the father of any man among you, but he is the messenger of Allah and the Seal of the Prophets; and Allah is ever Aware of all things. S. 33:40'" Pickthall or another T/L "Muhammad is not the father of any of your men, but he is the Apostle of Allah and the Last of the prophets; and Allah is cognizant of all things. S. 33:40" Shakir (T/L from the Koran) http://www.answering-islam.org/authors/shamoun/contact.html
[321] Surah 5:33 Pickthall T/L: "The only reward of those who make war upon Allah and His messenger and strive after corruption in the land will be that they will be killed or crucified, or have their hands and feet on alternate sides cut off, or will be expelled out of the land. Such will be their degradation in the world, and in the Hereafter theirs will be an awful doom;" See also http://www.answering-islam.org/Shamoun/cruelty.htm.
[322] "There is an ongoing discussion among scholars concerning the date and the pace of the process of Islamization in Palestine during the early Muslim period. Evidence concerning this subject is rare. Muslim sources relate that there was a substantial presence of Muslim in the area of Samaria from the tenth century onwards…presumed…result of immigration of Arab Muslims…(but) evidence found in a local Samaritan chronicle…small part of this Muslim population originated in Samaritan population which converted to Islam …as a result of difficult economic conditions…cannot be applied the Jewish and Christian communities." In www.jstor.org/stable/3632444. Article: *New Evidence Relating to the Process of Islamization in Palestine in the Early Muslim Period-The Case of Samaria* by Milka Levy-Rubin.
[323] "The Battle of Hattin took place on July 3 and 4, 1187, between the Crusader Kingdom of Jerusalem and the forces of the Kurdish Ayyubid sultan Salah ad-Din, known in the West as Saladin. It is also known as the Battle of the Horns of Hattin, from a nearby extinct volcano. The Muslim armies under Saladin captured or killed the vast majority of the Crusader forces, removing their capability to wage war.[9] As a direct result of the battle, Islamic forces once again became the eminent military power in the Holy Land, re-conquering Jerusalem and several other Crusader-held cities. These Christian defeats prompted the Third Crusade, which began two years after the Battle of Hattin." Wikipedia.
[324] "The Third Crusade (1189–1192), also known as The Kings' Crusade, was an attempt by European leaders to reconquer the Holy Land from Saladin (Ṣalāḥ ad-Dīn Yūsuf ibn Ayyūb). The campaign was largely successful, capturing the important cities of Acre and Jaffa, and reversing most of Saladin's conquests, but it failed to capture Jerusalem, the emotional and spiritual motivation of the Crusade… On 2 September 1192, following his defeat at Jaffa, Saladin was forced to finalize a treaty with Richard providing that Jerusalem would remain under Muslim control, while allowing unarmed Christian pilgrims and traders to visit the city. Ascalon was a contentious issue as it threatened communication between Saladin's dominions in Egypt and Syria; it was eventually agreed that Ascalon, with its defences demolished, be returned to Saladin's control. Richard departed the Holy Land on 9 October 1192." Wikipedia.
[325] "The Fourth Crusade (1202–04) was a Western European armed expedition originally intended to conquer Muslim-controlled Jerusalem by means of an invasion through Egypt. Instead, a sequence of events culminated in the Crusaders sacking the city of Constantinople, the capital of the Christian-controlled Byzantine Empire." Wikipedia.

1500-1917 AD In 1517 the Ottoman Empire took over control of Jerusalem. It maintained control till the end of WW1.[326] In the 1800-1900's there was a significant influx of Arabs (legal and illegal) into Samaria and other areas of Palestine.[327]

1917-1948 After WWI the areas controlled by the former Ottoman Empire were divided up. Samaria (and Judea) was entrusted to England from 1918 to 1948 by the Mandatory Palestine District of Samaria.

1948- Present After the conflict of 1948 most of Samaria was transferred to Jordanian oversight. In 1967 after the Six Day War it was brought under Israel control. This was codified in 1994 with the Israel-Jordan Treaty of Peace. In the Oslo Accord, of 1994, the Palestinian Liberation Organization (PLO) was given administration over certain parts of Jerusalem. The Jewish Shomun Regional Council still administers over the areas of the Jewish population in the Samarian area.

Conclusions:

1) The correct mountain, Mt. Moriah, is in Jerusalem. The adjustment to the text of the Torah by the Samaritans, which was in ancient times (as it was a problem in Jesus' day), was due to a contention between the priests of the Jews whom had remained in Samaria during the Assyrian and Babylonian captivities and the Jewish priests who returned at the end of the last captivity. Jesus clarified where the correct place was to worship.[328]

2) The Samaritan Jews mixed with the local populations, and accepted their polytheism early on. This brought the judgment of God upon them (the ten northern tribes) before the two southern tribes.[329] It even appears that later some Samaritans became Islamic during the Early Islamic Period, as a result of economic pressure.[330] For these reasons they were and have been despised by the Jews who returned from Babylon after the Captivity and those who have returned in more modern times.

3) The presence of the Jewish people in Ancient Samaria is well established, and there is evidence of Arabic intrusion into Samaria in the Early Islamic Period but not before. It is probable that the modern Palestinian Arabs are unrelated to the people groups of ancient Samaria, but were part of groups that

---

[326] "At the outset of the Ottoman era, an estimated 1,000 Jewish families lived in the country, mainly Jerusalem, Nablus (Shechem), Hebron, Gaza, Safad (Tzfat) and the villages of Galilee. The community was comprised of Jews who had never left the Land as well as immigrants from North Africa and Europe… " Sultan Suleiman the Magnificent promoted Jewish improvements but other leaders after him did not. The Jews became tenant farmers and their situation did not improve till the late 1800's-early 1900's with advent of Christian from England and the US missionary endeavors in the area. As well, there was an increased interest in archaeology of the area. The Jewish population increased. Per the authors the stage was being set for the Zionist Movement.   http://www.jewishvirtuallibrary.org/jsource/History/Ottoman.html

[327] Between 1800 and 1914, the Muslim population had a yearly average increase in the order of magnitude of roughly 6-7 per thousand… *It is possible that part of the growth of the Muslim population was due to immigration.*" Roberto Bachi, *The Population of Israel* (Jerusalem: Institute of Contemporary Jewry, Hebrew University, 1974), p. 45. Quoted in http://www.meforum.org/522/the-smoking-gun-arab-immigration-into-palestine.

[328] See discussion between Jesus Christ and the woman at the well. (John 4:5-29)

[329] "The Samaritan community, which numbered more than a million in late Roman times and only 146 in 1917, numbers today about 640 people representing four large families. They are culturally different from both Jewish and non-Jewish populations in the Middle East and their origin remains a question of great interest. Genetic differences between the Samaritans and neighboring Jewish and non-Jewish populations are corroborated in the present study … Principal component analysis suggests a common ancestry of Samaritan and Jewish patrilineages. Most of the former may be traced back to a common ancestor in the paternally-inherited Jewish high priesthood (Cohanim) at the time of the Assyrian conquest of the kingdom of Israel.
Hum Mutat 24:248–260, 2004. r 2004 Wiley-Liss, Inc." www.rabbinics.org/classical/05%20Samaritans%20DNA.pdf

[330] About 600-700 A.D. See previous references as well recording economic pressure on Samaritans.

were shifted to Palestinian Samaria during several periods including the Ottoman Period and even more modern times.[331]

Please note that this short review on Samaria is not meant to be a complete document regarding the history this complex region, but rather to show its influence on the Jewish people and to document the Jews' historicity in the region.

Samaria and Mount Gerizim

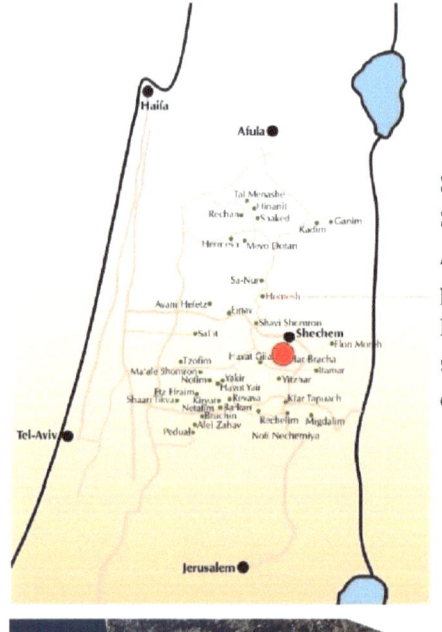

Samaria modern Shomron_map by Appleville on wiki public domain 11-30-15 Mount Gerizim is just south of Shechem. Red dot added by JGL.

Nasa satallite image of Haifa, the Sea of Galilee, the Jordan Valley and Samaria public domain. It corresponds to above map.

---

[331] See text.

Images: Samaria Samaritans and Mt. Gerizim

Samaritan Priest and the Samaritan Torah photo 1903

Mount Gerizim from Mount Ebal looking south across valley where Shechem (modern Nablus) is located. Dated 1890-1900. From: http://www.biblewalks.com/Sites/Mount Gerizim.html online 12-25-15.

The Sacrificing of the lamb during Passover at Mt Gerizim by Samaritan priests. photo marked 1931.

Ruins of the capital of Samaria from ancient times. Picture 1925 public domain from Wikipedia 12-25-15.

Coins Representative of Samaria Descriptions

Row 1: Phoenician-Sidon: 1/8 shekel Obv. Persian king battling a lion; Rev. war galley to left 100-200 BC. Meshorer #96.

Row 2: AR (silver) obol of Attica, Athens: Obv. Athena with helmet; Rev. owl standing right with AOE with olive spray and crescent behind. About 300-400 BC.

Row 3: AR (silver) obol Philisto-Arabian of Gaza. Obv. Owl with AOE, Rev. crude Athena female head to right in barbaric style-well worn. 400-330 BC.

Row 4: Neopolis with Severus Alexander. Obv. Head positioned to the right with countermark. Rev. Mt. Gerizim with a temple on top and clouds tumbling down the mountain. Stairs are in the center. Drawing to the right.

Samaria Coins

Phoenician-Sidon
300-400 BC

Greek Attica Athens
300-400 BC similar to
Samarian ones of the period.

Philistine-Gaza
300-400 BC

Mt Gerizim with the temple on it. Coin of
Alexander Severus 338 AD

True/False Religions Portrayed in Coins

As has been discussed, coins often reflect the political views of the leaders having the coins stamped. Economic progress, extension of their societies, and finally the underlying religious views by which they justify their existence are reflected in their coins. Both Judaism and Christianity have contended to be heard among the plethora of religions. However, the Bible states that "many are those who follow the broad way to destruction and few who find the narrow way." This is reflected in the coinage of the nations.

Row 1: On the right is the motif of the false religion of Zeus who was the chief of the Greek gods. He is seen in a tetra-style temple. As was typical of Greek gods he could be capricious and cruel. On the left side is a coin reflecting the True God in the façade of the temple on a coin from the Bar Kochba War stamped on a modern Jewish medal. The conservative Jews in ancient times portrayed images of many religious themes: menorah, table of showbread, Jerusalem Temple, grapes and grapes leaves, but not images of animals or humans. The 2nd Commandment forbade this. It should be noted that the Herods, and some modern Jewish leaders rejected and now reject this view and have placed human images on their coins.

Row 2: The right shows the implements of the Roman priest. These tools were involved in the rituals of divining coursed of action by reading the entrails and liver of animals that had been sacrificed, with libations of wine poured over the animals. The entrails were then separated out using the cutting instruments and a determination was made based on this, much like reading Tarot cards. This was in stark contrast to the guiding light of the Holy and Pure God. When sacrifices were made to Him it was not for guidance but for the propitiation of sins, as the Bible says, "the soul that sins must die." Animals' blood only covered sins, but Christ's blood removes them. Ancient and modern Jewish images portray Temple items like the Menorah which gave light in the Holy, and Holy of Holies places and is analogous to the light of God's Spirit within believer's in Him.

Row 3: Many secular coins glorify man and the coin on the right reflects this with the image of Nero on one side and on the reverse a town which had been named Sepphoris but which was changed to Neronia to exalt Nero. In contrast to this is a Byzantine coin on the left which reads "King of Kings and Lord of Lords" referring to Jesus Christ. As Jesus was a man, it may not be a violation to portray His image, though He is God; or it may not be appropriate. I am not sure on this point. As well, many Byzantine leaders did not follow Jesus Christ's teachings.

True And False Religions Portrayed In Coins

Jewish/
Christian

Roman

The Orphic Egg vs. the True Creator God

The Orphic Egg is an excellent example of how the minds of mankind can distort reality in such a fashion as the view obtained allows them to be their own gods, deciding on good vs. evil. The glorious concepts of a Creator God who is only one, righteous, holy, truth, and all powerful are rejected. It is clear even from a limited human understanding that if there is absolute "truth" or any of the other traits that are listed above, then it cannot be relative to each individual's opinion. If all "truth" is relative, then there are no foundations upon which to judge right and wrong, and man does what is right in each owns eyes.[332] Any society which adheres to no absolute values will degenerate; and to have absolute values requires one who is all supreme, the Creator, to determine those values. Our responsibility is to find the true Creator and obey Him. The Greek and Roman leaders by in large did not desire to know Him but worshiped grotesque gods and goddesses. They accepted an evolutionary beginning of all things so as to justify their beliefs. The Orphic Egg was such a belief; and yet it was accepted in otherwise technologically sophisticated societies.

"The **Orphic Egg** in the Ancient Greek Orphic tradition is the cosmic egg from which hatched the primordial hermaphroditic deity Phanes/Protogonus… The egg is often depicted with a serpent wound about it…The egg symbolizes the belief in the Greek Orphic religion that the universe originated from within a silver egg. The first emanation from this egg, described in an ancient hymn, was Phanes-Dionysus, the personification of light…In Greek myth, particularly Orphic thought, Phanes is the golden winged Primordial Being who was hatched from the shining Cosmic Egg that was the source of the universe. Called Protogonos (First-Born) and Eros (Love) — being the seed of gods and men — Phanes means "Manifestor" or "Revealer," and is related to the Greek words "light" and 'to shine forth.'" From: Wikipedia "Orphic Egg."

Note the vast contrast to how the Bible describes God, Yahweh, who is outside the creation and simply speaks it into existence. There are no multiple gods within the created universe whom war with each other, and are often as capricious as mankind itself. Even the concept of light is distorted as it comes forth from the "hatched" Phanes. The Bible says that God is Light and in Him there is no darkness at all. This light is from outside the creation (as it was present before the sun and stars etc. see Genesis 1:3,14). As well, a serpent encompasses the egg. In most cultures of the earth a serpent represents evil. The Bible clearly refers to Satan as a serpent. Again, this is a distortion as it implies that the serpent had or has control of the creation, which is not true. It should be noted that all mankind has had the teaching of the early chapters of Genesis (1-8) given to them, but as people groups moved away from worshiping the True God their knowledge of the true beginnings became confounded. They began to worship the creation rather than the Creator. Yet, the true Creator continued throughout man's history to reveal His power, holiness, and righteousness through the prophets of the Jewish people.

---

[332] Judges 17:6 "In those days there was no king in Israel, but every man did that which was **right** in his own eyes."

True and False Religions Continued
The Orphic Egg vs. a Holy God

The Orphic Egg on a Altar with Snakes surrounding it.

Caracalla Roman Emperor image bust to right

A Lulav (myrtle/palm branch/willow bound together) with etrogs on sides. Used during Succoth. Inscription Year 4.

Chalice with Pearl rim. Inscription "To the redemption of Zion." Struck 69 A.D.

Smelting Metal (Iron) in Ancient Persia and Egypt

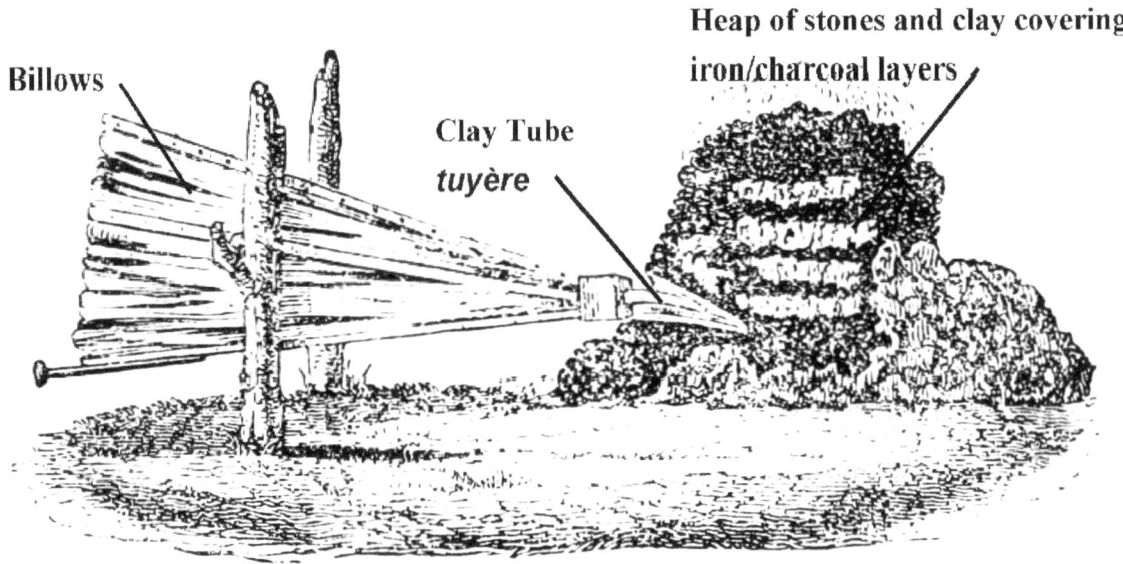

Fig. 1. Persian Method of Smelting Iron.

The simplest process known for obtaining iron from its ore can be carried out in an ordinary blacksmith's fire by throwing crushed ore upon the ignited fuel, covering it with coal, and, after urging the fire with bellows for a considerable time, there will be found in the bottom of the fire an irregular mass of forgeable metal...In Fig.1 is shown a modification of this process, practiced by the iron-workers of Persia and adjacent countries, who have manufactured both iron and steel by this simple and inexpensive method (as measured by their standards of the value of time, labor, and material), from the days of Tubal-Cain to the present time...

A basin-shaped hole, six to twelve inches in depth and twelve to twenty-four inches in diameter, was first made in the earth; this cavity was then lined with moistened charcoal dust, which was well rammed to make it as dense as possible; the hearth thus formed was then filled with charcoal, on which was placed a layer of crushed ore, and over this alternate layers of fuel and ore untilthe heap was of the desired height; the outside of the mass of charcoal and ore was then incased in a covering of rough stones laid in a mortar of clay and sand, or, in some cases, it was merely plastered over with a thick layer of such mortar; care was always taken to have a hole near the bottom, just above the edge of the hearth, for the insertion of a tube of baked clay to serve as a *tuyère*, and a second hole at the top for the escape of smoke and gases. Fire was then introduced at the tuyere and the bellows connected; a gentle blast being used until all the moisture in the ore and the covering of the heap was driven off. As soon as this was accomplished, the blast was increased and the heat thereby augmented. At the end of several hours a mass of metallic iron, weighing twenty or thirty pounds, was found in the bottom of the hearth, from which it was removed by tongs and forged by sledge-hammers into the desired shape, several reheatings being required. The iron obtained was not usually over twenty per cent of that in the ore, and only the richest ores were used.

From: THE DEVELOPMENT OF AMERICAN INDUSTRIES SINCE COLUMBUS.I. EARLY STEPS IN IRON-MAKING. Popular Mechanics December 1890. By WILLIAM F. DURFEE, Engineer.

Raw Metals Used in Smelting or Hammering

Malleable Gold

Malleable Silver

Malleable Copper

High Grade Iron Ore

Electrum

"Electrum consists primarily of gold and silver but is sometimes found with traces of platinum, copper, and other metals. The name is mostly applied informally to compositions between about 20-80% gold and 20-80% silver atoms, but these are strictly called gold or silver depending on the dominant element…Analysis of the composition of electrum in ancient Greek coinage dating from about 600 BC shows that the gold content was about 55.5% in the coinage issued by Phocaea."[333] Deposits of electrum were found naturally and were malleable so that simple stamping could be done before smelting was perfected.

1/24 Electrum Stater from Ionia dated about 600 B.C. Size is 7 mm and 0.58 gm.[334]

Malleable gold nuggets (probably electrum).

---

[333] https://en.wikipedia.org/wiki/Electrum
[334] Information per CNG coins. https://www.cngcoins.com/

Clay Coin Forger's Mold
(Byzantine Time Period)

Below is an image of one section of a clay mold, when stacked together with other ones (see drawing), is used to cast forger's coins. There is a small slot (not seen in this mold) which allows the hot, liquid metal to be poured into the mold. Once cooled, with the mold pulled apart, the coin edge with its small flange is then filed off. Each mold has a convex and a concave side.(1,2,3) Below is an example of Maximinus 4/5th Century AD.

(Concave on left and convex on right)

Flange File Marks

Stacked clay molds with pour site for molten metal facing in image

1) These are comments from a coin website regarding a clay mould similar to mine.
http://www.coincommunity.com/forum/topic.asp?TOPIC_ID=195104

2) FORGER'S COIN MOLD, TERRACOTTA, 286 AD AND LATER 286 AD AND LATER. Forgers's coin mold made of terracota and featuring the obverse of a follis of Maximianus and the reverse depicts Genius. These molds are frequently found in Egypt. https://www.vcoins.com/fr/stores/barry_and_darling/20/product/forgers_coin_mold_terracotta_286_ad_and_later_286_ad_and_later/538912/Default.aspx

3) http://www.nederlandsemunten.nl/ photograph of stacked clay molds from which drawing was made.

Scriptures Relating to the Messiah

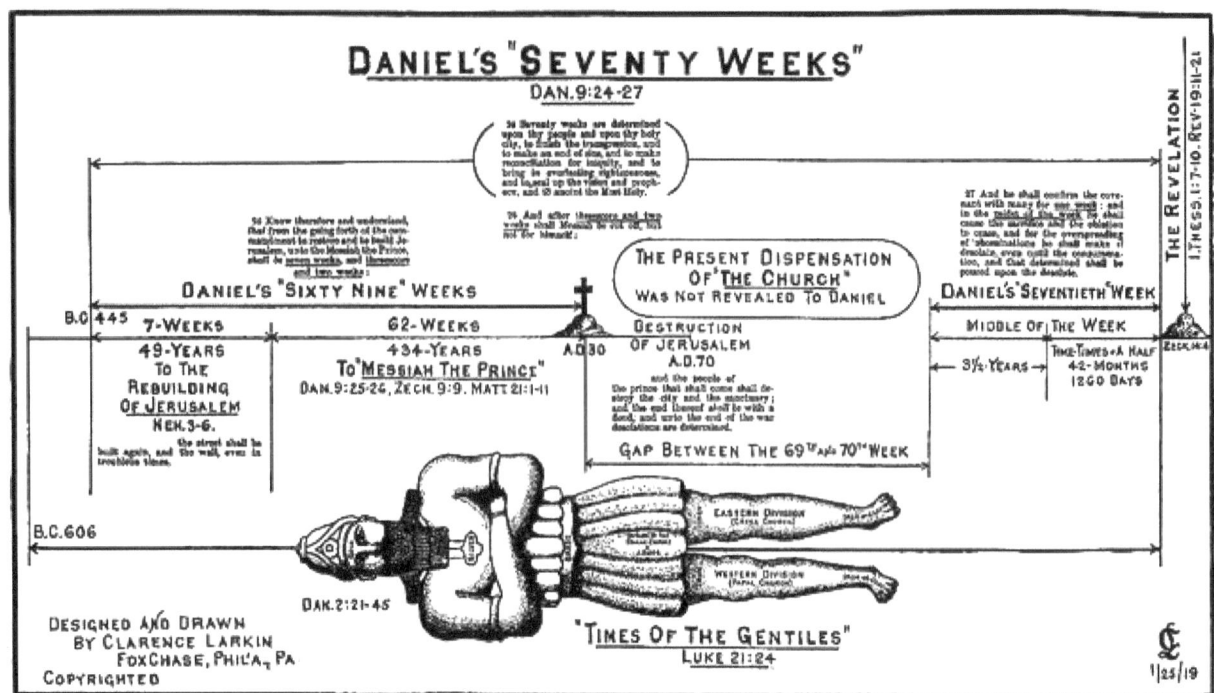

Daniel 9: [1] In the first year of Darius the son of Ahasuerus, of Median descent, who was made king over the kingdom of the Chaldeans [2] in the first year of his reign, I, Daniel, observed in the books the number of the years which was *revealed as* the word of the LORD to Jeremiah the prophet for the completion of the desolations of Jerusalem, *namely*, seventy years. ... [26] Then after the sixty-two weeks the Messiah will be cut off and have nothing, and the people of the prince who is to come will destroy the city and the sanctuary. And its end *will come* with a flood; even to the end there will be war; desolations are determined.

Luke 21: [10] Then He continued by saying to them, "Nation will rise against nation and kingdom against kingdom, [11] and there will be great earthquakes, and in various places plagues and famines; and there will be terrors and great signs from heaven. [12] "But before all these things, they will lay their hands on you and will persecute you, delivering you to the synagogues and prisons, bringing you before kings and governors for My name's sake. ... [20] "But when you see Jerusalem surrounded by armies, then recognize that her desolation is near. [21] Then those who are in Judea must flee to the mountains, and those who are in the midst of the city must leave, and those who are in the country must not enter the city; [22] because these are days of vengeance, so that all things which are written will be fulfilled. ... [27] Then they will see THE SON OF MAN COMING IN A CLOUD with power and great glory. [28] But when these things begin to take place, straighten up and lift up your heads, because your redemption is drawing near.

Matthew 26: [64] Jesus said to him, "You have said it *yourself*; nevertheless I tell you, hereafter you will see THE SON OF MAN SITTING AT THE RIGHT HAND OF POWER, and COMING ON THE CLOUDS OF HEAVEN."

(Larkin chart 1918: public domain)

He Is Risen

Matthew 28 ¹Now after the Sabbath, as it began to dawn toward the first *day* of the week, Mary Magdalene and the other Mary came to look at the grave. ² And behold, a severe earthquake had occurred, for an angel of the Lord descended from heaven and came and rolled away the stone and sat upon it. ³ And his appearance was like lightning, and his clothing as white as snow. ⁴ The guards shook for fear of him and became like dead men. ⁵ The angel said to the women, "Do not be afraid; for I know that you are looking for Jesus who has been crucified.

⁶ He is not here, for He has risen, just as He said."

What Must I do to be Saved?

The Creator's Plan for You

Ancient writings and all cultures of the world teach about the Creator, a worldwide flood which destroyed the surface of the earth because of the sins of man, and the need of a blood sacrifice to atone for these sins to be at peace with Almighty God.

The sacred scriptures of the bible teach that as a man Jesus Christ came from God, to die as the blood payment for all men's sins, and that whoever accepted his sacrifice for their sins would be forgiven of them. As God, Christ Jesus could then give them new life, by recreating the hearts of those forgiven. They could then live eternally with God now and after death.

Would you like to do this? If so, the **AACTS** steps below are suggested:

1) The book of Romans 3:23 says, "For all have sinned' (disobeyed) 'and fall short of the glory of God." **Admit** that you have sinned.

2) Romans 6:23 states, "For the wages of sin is death, but the free gift of God is eternal life in Christ Jesus our Lord." **Acknowledge** that sin is leading you to death (physically, emotionally, spiritually), and turn to God.

3) Romans 10:9-10 says, "That if you **Confess** with your mouth Jesus as Lord, and believe in your heart that God raised him from the dead, you shall be saved; for with the heart man believes resulting in righteousness" (right standing with God) "and with the mouth he confesses resulting in salvation" (freed forever from the punishment of sin). If you confess the **Teachings** of the bible, that Jesus is Lord and he died for your sins you will experience **Salvation.**

So **AACTS** now! And get involved in a local church that teaches the bible.

Quotations from the NAS bible used with permission Deluge 2000

ABOUT THE AUTHOR

Dr. John G. Leslie graduated with a BS (Biology) from American University, Washington, DC (1973), a Ph.D. in Experimental Pathology from the University of Utah School of Medicine (1980), a Doctorate of Medicine at Oral Roberts University (1989) and Residency in Internal Medicine/Pediatrics from the University of Oklahoma - Tulsa Branch (1993). He has been Board Certified in Pediatrics and Internal Medicine. He also has a Bible School Certificate of Completion from the Word of Faith Bible College, Dallas, Texas (1982), and a PhD in Archaeology and Biblical History, Trinity Southwest University, Albuquerque (2012).

He has worked with several leading scientists both in the United States and abroad. He has been an author in publications such as The New England Journal of Medicine, Biochemical and Biophysical Research Communications, Connective Tissue Research, and others including foreign journals. He has written communications in several newspapers including the American Medical Association News, and The American Academy of Pediatric News. Articles have appeared in Ex Nihilo and in its Technical Journal issues. His human bone studies have been reported in the Trinity Southwest University publications regarding the excavation of Tall el Hammam, Jordan. It is considered a possible site of the Biblical Sodom.

He is or has been a member of the West Coast Connective Tissue Society (USA), Australian-New Zealand Connective Tissue Society, American Medical Association, Tulsa Medical Society, New Mexico Medical Society, Christian Medical Society, Pro Life Victoria (Australia), Creation Research Society, Oklahomans for Life, New Mexico Right to Life, American Academy for Medical Ethics, and the Phi Theta Kappa Honor Society. He has been awarded a Ewing Foundation Student Fellowship (1987) for oncology research, and he was an Eagle Scout in the Boy Scouts of America.

His early work involved protein structure and function studies. He then pursued studies in protein metabolism. Further studies included the development of monoclonal antibodies to various biologically active proteins. He has investigated the structure of DNA in certain cancers. At present, he works as a physician in a rural community and has participated in an annual archaeological dig in Jordan.

You can visit the author's website at **www.DefendingTheChristianFaith.org**

To God Be the Glory

www.ingramcontent.com/pod-product-compliance
Lightning Source LLC
Chambersburg PA
CBHW041541220426
43664CB00002B/18